With Crew #13
A History of B-17
with the 100th Boi
& A Visit Back to Thorpe Abbotts

Third Printing, Special Edition
Original Copyright ©1990
Third Printing ©2004
All Rights Reserved
Earl Benham
Phoenix, Arizona

ISBN 1-4196-8525-2

Written by Earl Benham
Cover and book design by Scott Smith

This story is dedicated to:

My Flight Crew #13

Our Ground Crew

The 100th Bomb Group

The B-17s We Flew

The 8th Air Force

The Fighter Plane Escort

Forward

The story of "With Crew #13" is unique in the fact it describes the events of an Air force Flight Crew from the start of their selection as a crew, continuing on through their training program in the United States and through their actual experiences on aerial combat over Germany in World War II.

Flying the B-17 Flying Fortresses of that era with the Eighth Air Force and with the 100th Bomb Group, the 350th Bomb Squadron at the base at Thorpe Abbotts, England.

The records of their combat flights listed here are authentic as to dates and missions, described in authentic detail.

This story indicates the true details and some indications of the efforts of the men of the combat flight crews. Men whose service was very instrumental in the conclusion of World War II.

To these men this story applies and how the author was involved as Radio Operator on the Flying Fortress with Crew #13.

– Earl Benham

Preface

This story starts as I arrive a Moses Lake, Washington. The operational training base for the new combat crews. This was the late spring of 1943.

I had previously graduated from Radio school at Scott Field, Illinois. I had previously graduated from the Gunnery School at Harlingen, Texas. We were here to organize our flight crews, and start on an incredible journey which proved to be a lifetime of excitement and experience compressed into a time period of a few months.

The story of these events is written in the following pages, much has been forgotten over the past many years. The only guide I have, except for my memories, is a diary I kept while flying combat missions.

Only a small portion of the experiences can be written here. Our personal conversations and actions may be referred to only briefly, as personal choices must be respected. I have no right to explain or comment on the private conversations and actions of the men involved here.

Just to say *"we were a great crew"* will have to suffice in a non-personal commentary. As we flew these many hours in training and in combat, we developed a certain friendship and respect for each member of our crew.

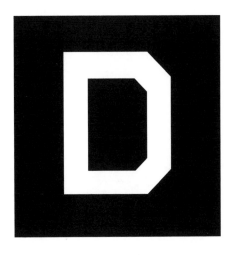

The Tail insignia of the 100th Bomb Group

Squadron codes

349th   XR
350th   LN
351st   EP
418th   LD

Contents

Arriving at Moses Lake, Washington in the late spring of 1943, I was fortunate in being assigned to a tar papered barracks. Some of the men had to erect tents, not enough barracks were ready on the day we arrived. As bleak as the tar papered barracks were, they were better than tents. The ground at Moses Lake was hard and rocky, a big effort to drive in tent stakes.

The Radio School and offices were not completely operational. It was a dismal looking place.

After a few orientation lectures and a few days later, we were divided into groups of ten men. Men from all parts of the country seemed to be assembled here.

All were trained in their particular part of a flight crew. All had met the requirements necessary to be qualified for flight training. I thought of the many men I had seen in various schools I had attended, that had not met these qualifications. Many disappointed young men had failed to reach the point we were at here at Moses Lake.

We were now selected for our ten man crew. We had no choice in this selection, we were all strangers at this time. We later became well acquainted. I flew all of my combat missions with this very crew. All except for the co-pilot, we had several co-pilots until we started our combat tour with Lt. Ogg who we met at our base in England.

I believe as a crew we became more than just friends. While during our flying career, we developed a certain respect for each crew member. After being selected as a flight crew we were ready to start our flight training. Each of us would finally be using the skills we had been taught in various schools we had attended prior to this time. These skills we soon found were quite inadequate, much more had to be understood. We all had much to become familiar with.

Our First Training Flight.

The day arrived when we reported for our first flight as a crew of a B-17 Flying Fortress. On this flight, our pilot was checked out as first pilot of our crew. He had a total of six hours of four engine flying time. A command pilot instructor was with him on this check flight.

My duty was to check out the radio equipment for take off. I remember it took me longer than I wanted. I could now understand this was not classroom work. My duty on the flight was to contact the ground station at proper intervals using Morse code and the procedure we had been instructed to use. This was only a training flight and would be the first of many flights.

We made a nice takeoff. As we climbed to about 4,000 feet altitude I noticed the air was quite turbulent. The pilots were checking out various maneuvers, some were rough, such as 45 and 90 degree banking turns.

After about two hours of this type flying I became air sick. I signed off the radio and went out of the radio room to a smoother place to ride in the B-17. We landed after a four hour flight. I took my papers and equipment back to the office. We all then went to chow and had a good meal.

Up to this date we were all inexperienced flyers, some crew members were very troubled by motion sickness, while others were not.

Other Incidents at Moses Lake.
We were informed we were going to have a three phase, or three month stage of flight training. This would take about five months to complete and be ready to go overseas.

At this time we did not know what theater of operations we would go to. Either Africa, South Pacific, Italy or England. We did know Moses Lake would be our first phase of training. The other locations of our phase training were unknown to us at this time.

After this first flight we were on a regular schedule of four hours flight time each day, weather permitting, and if an airplane was available for us to use. We had several B-17s at this base. Not all were operational at all times.

Air sickness continued to bother me. I knew if I could

not overcome this I would be grounded and off the flight crew. I took the effort of spending some of my "off time" sitting in the airplane while on the ground, either reading or checking the equipment. I was trying to associate the smell of the plane with something other than air sickness. This effort paid off, I soon corrected my problem. Many men could not overcome air sickness and were out of the flight training program.

Many incidents, or unusual events occurred almost every day. One especially interesting to me, I will recall it here.

We were flying a pilot test flight. The only crew members aboard were the flight engineer, myself, the two pilots, one being the instructor pilot. I had completed my first contact with the ground station and had some time on my hands. I went into the nose of the plane and was lying face down enjoying the scenery of the ground far below. Suddenly I was floating weightless in air, then a moment later I was pinned to the floor. This experience was caused by some difficult maneuvers the pilots were doing. They had put the plane in a dive, then a sharp pull out. This caused my weightless sensation, as well as the G-Force that pinned me down on the floor as they pulled out of the dive.

This experience only happened this one time in my flying career. My thought at the time was of the equipment in the radio room. We had the hatch open over the

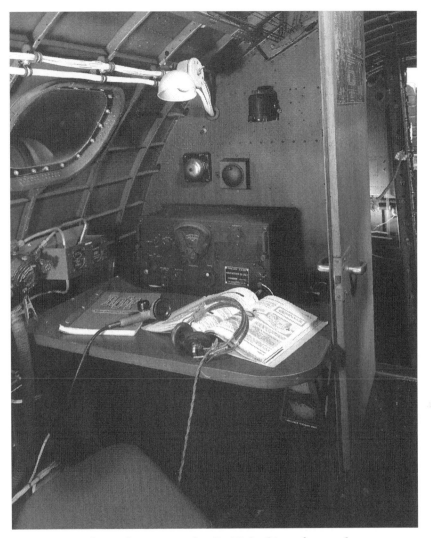

The radio room of a B-17 looking forward.

radio room. I visualized items floating out of the open hatch. Upon inspection I found my parachute rolled up in a corner. No loss or damage to any of the equipment.

Our crew members were all new at their positions. I was becoming more and more confident of our pilot. I later learned he was a man of cool nerve and logic. This attribute was necessary in the vicious tactics of aerial combat, which I knew we may someday encounter.

Starting our Second Phase at Geiger Field, Spokane, Washington.

Our first phase of training was completed with too many incidents to recall at this writing. We went to Geiger Field for the next exciting phase.

Geiger was a well equipped field, more complicated than Moses Lake. This extra equipment was appreciated for our 2nd phase of training.

Our schedule here was to include some night flying. Our flight time was to rotate around the clock. This schedule would change our habits of early morning rising and the old custom of having meals, morning, noon and evening, and having the nights as free time.

We usually had briefings for all flights and often a brief physical before take-offs. The flights were practice for all crew members. I think we all enjoyed the gunnery flights more than any other flights.

A gunnery range had been developed. This range was about 15 miles long with targets on the ground along the way. The course was winding and we flew at full speed (170 mph), at low altitude as low as 10 feet above the ground. As we approached the end of the course we would lift to about 1,000 feet and make a 180 degree turn and again run the target course.

This was all fun and exciting for us young men involved. The pilots also took turns firing the side guns. Side guns (waist guns) were the only ones we used on these low targets. We often asked "who is flying the airplane?" who cares was usually the answer.

By this time I noticed we had a great crew. Certainly no "*C.S.*" which we had been accustomed to in the training schools.

On one flight we "bombed" Grand Coulee dam. At the time I was busy on the radio and missed seeing it. I thought perhaps someday I would return by car to the that area and see the dam site. Many years later my wife and were able to do that very thing.

Our flights were often over the beautiful Wenatchee Valley. Many years later my wife and I also returned to that area by car.

Our phase training at Geiger was coming to an end, again so many incidents of interest occurred recalling them all would be near impossible. I did not keep a diary of any of this training, much to my regret later.

I recall one special lecture we had at Geiger. This lecture was given by a General who had recently returned from a combat tour in Africa. His purpose was to inform us as well las he could of combat conditions in that area and others.

He started his address with an unusual statement by saying..."*Are there any men here who would prefer to be off flying status?* If so just sign the release forms, you will not be penalized, but you will then be out of the flying program. We do not want men on flight crews who would prefer to not be here."

Not one man signed the release. We were all volunteers and remained to stay that way. Later in training we could not drop out as easily, which is understandable as we needed a strong solid organization. They did give us a chance to leave.

It was now into the month of August 1943. We were ready for our first furlough. On the night flight just prior to this furlough, and just prior to take off, S/Sgt. Goodman said jokingly, "*now if we can make this flight without a crash we will have our furlough*". On that night flight, we had an engine malfunction and landed with three engines, no problem but we had never had this happen before.

I took the train to Minnesota. Commercial flying was expensive and not too reliable as to schedules in that day and age. My six day furlough went by rapidly, visiting my parents and friends. On this furlough I visited my Grandmother for the last time. She seemed quite well and advised me *"whatever you do, do not let them put you in an airplane!"* She never knew that I was a flight crew member, at least I never thought she knew. She passed away before I returned from England after my tour.

After the furlough, we returned to Geiger and made a few flights before finishing our second phase of flight training.

I remember one flight I made. This was a special trip with only the two pilots and the engineer and myself aboard. We flew to Pendelton to pick up a few men who were returning to Geiger. The man riding in the radio room with me suddenly looked terrified as we were making our landing approach to Geiger. I asked him what his problem was. He said *"he had recently been hospitalized because of a crash landing they had made."* His nerves seemed to be bothering him at this time.
I doubt he ever returned to flying status.

We were now well into the month of August. Ready to start our third phase at Pendelton, Oregon.

Our Final Phase at Pendelton, Oregon.
Flying out of Pendelton was routine. We had one exceptional flight. This one was directed out over the Pacific

Ocean. I will explain the details here.

We were to fly west to the coast and then proceed out 500 miles over the Pacific, then make a 90 degree turn south. Proceed 100 then turn 90 degrees to the east and return to the coast, intersecting our initial starting point.

My schedule on the flight was to contact the ground station each hour and give our position report. Perhaps every half hour, I don't recall which. This was wanted by Air Sea Rescue.

After we had flown out about 400 miles, the transmission to the mainland were too weak. I needed to extend my long ranged "trailing wire" antenna. This was a mechanism which ran electrically a reel of antenna wire. I would let out the amount of antenna necessary to resonate the transmitter. In this process I had a malfunction and the wire jerked and the eight pound ball on the end of the wire fell off. I could not extend the antenna. I had no way to transmit our position to the base. The Air Sea Rescue became a bit excited until they finally heard from us as we neared the coast.

On this flight we passed an ocean going freighter going in the opposite direction. We flew so low beside it as we passed, I could look up to see the sailors standing by their railing, waving as we passed.

One other spectacular flight was in the area of Mt. Adams, Mt. Hood and Mt. Rainier. All were visible at one time from our plane. We probably were at 6000 feet. This was a great sight for me as I had never seen mountains to any great extent. This would have been a great sight for anyone.

Grand Island, Nebraska.

When our phase at Pendelton ended, we boarded a train en route to our next destination, which was Grand Island, Nebraska. The trip seemed unending on the slow train.

We arrived at the base at Grand Island about 2 a.m. The base was mostly closed at that time of day. A sergeant opened the barracks with beds and a mattress rolled upon each bed. No people in the supply room to give us bedding.

I was tired as we all were, there was no food either. I went to sleep on top of the mattress and was soon awakened by swarms of mosquitoes. I pulled an extra mattress on top of myself and went back to sleep.

No comforts of home, but I thought much better than the men in the south Pacific were having. I felt we perhaps had nothing to complain about.

Our airplanes arrived within a few days. What we done prior to their arrival I don't recall. No passes to town were allowed. We started to test fly the planes, testing the new equipment by making several flights in the

Grand Island area. Many flights at very low altitudes, just skinning over the tree tops.

The farmers didn't like this as their chickens weren't laying their quota of eggs, due to the noisy aircraft overhead. Therefore an order was issued by the High Command to ban this type of flying, we had enjoyed it very much.

We were at Grand Island about three weeks, I am not certain of the length of our stay there. The rumor at the time was, the airplanes were to be left at Grand Island. We were in a state of confusion because we had been told we would fly them to England. That is the way we wanted to go.

Leaving Grand Island for Bangor, Maine.
The Air Force Command had some indecision as to how we were to proceed from Grand Island. It was rumored once we would go to New York by train and then to England by ship. We loaded into trucks for a ride to the station. However, this was canceled. We gratefully returned to the barracks. We once were issued jungle equipment. This was returned at once. We gratefully returned it. Apparently a mistake in some order.

Within a few days we were again assigned to our airplanes and briefed for a flight to Bangor, Maine, which was to be the first leg of our trip to England. A few moments before takeoff, (we were in the plane ready to go) the flight was canceled. These false starts happened three times, some in orders along the command caused us a three day delay in takeoff. We never knew why. Some of the men of the crews had wives, relatives or friends waiting to see them off. One can imagine their reaction to this indecision. We finally left for Bangor.

The flight to Bangor was made a bit more exciting as we detoured from our regular flight path and made a low pass "buzz job" over Oskaloosa, Iowa. The home town of our pilot Van. His parents and wife were standing out in their lawn looking up as we flew over. We were so low I looked up to see the tops of the trees as we passed. We circled the town, I can remember people looking up at us. The school children out in the school yard looking up.

Many years late, I heard the famous news reporter Steve Bell lived in that town at the time. He was a grade student, perhaps was in the school yard as we flew over. Thirty years later I wrote to him and received an answer saying he seemed to recall that event.

We flew on to Wisconsin and flew over the home town of our navigator, Harold Becker. I was busy on the radio and didn't see the town. Tragically, our navigator was killed on a flight to Berlin on May of the following year. May 7th 1944. Mentioned later in this story.

On this long flight to Bangor, it was necessary for me to

again use the trailing wire antenna for the long range communication with Grand Island. There were times as we changed altitude, I was not aware of the change and should I have the long wire out, the eight pound ball at the end of the wire could hit something on the ground. I asked the flight engineer to call me on the interphone if we should be going to these very low altitudes.

The engineer had a decided southern accent he would call and say *"is yo' trailin' wire in?"* We carried this expression as time went on, even as a joke. If someone was going out on a pass, we would sometimes ask "is yo' trailin' wire in?" I doubt if this ever became an ETO expression, we enjoyed it somewhat.

Leaving Bangor for Goose Bay, LaBrador.
Then on to Greenland.

We completed our flight to Bangor, landing late afternoon and were informed the next leg of our journey would be Goose Bay, LaBrador. My briefing as radio operator was routine except a strong report on the safety aspects.

The flight route was over very desolate country. An airplane down in that area would be hard to locate unless the radio operator had previously sent the accurate position reports, which he had been given by the navigator. We did not have radar control. Our Morse code was the only long range communication with the ground stations.

The flight to Goose Bay was uneventful, no emergencies of any type. Our stay at Bangor had only been overnight.

The strange scenery of Goose Bay was hardly noticed by us at this time. We had seen so many rapid changes of environment and were becoming accustomed to changes. Our stay at Goose Bay was two days, the next stop would be Greenland.

An incident happened to a crew the day before we left. A crew we had known while in training. They were on their way to Greenland when a propeller fell off one their engines of their plane. This huge propeller could have done serious damage to their plane.

They knew it was falling off, the radio operator told me he frantically sent out the distress S.O.S. distress signal. He jokingly said he *"alerted the entire world"*. They were fortunate and landed back at Goose Bay safely.

One of the other planes had collided with a corner of a building as they were taxiing for take off to Greenland. There were problems, and more problems it seemed.

The base at Greenland was called "Bluie West 1" or just B.W.1. It was located on the southern end of Greenland. This would be our first over water flight on this trip to England. I had quite an intense briefing, especially on the safety procedures. The sending out S.O.S. signals if necessary, etc.

With high hopes for a nice ride, we left Goose Bay.
I had some feeling of apprehension as I realized I had
the responsibility of sending the position should we be
forced down in the cold water of the North Atlantic.

We were not radar controlled and the possibility that my
radio transmissions would not be received by anyone if
I should not have my transmitter in proper order.
We didn't have push button radio operation in that era.
There was also jamming of our frequencies by German
submarines and other interferences, because we used low
frequencies.

I had never been faced with this challenge prior to this
flight. However, the flight to Greenland turned out to be
only routine. The sight of icebergs was spectacular to us.

The airfield at Greenland (B.W.1.) was nestled in a basin
with medium sized mountains on three sides, a long
narrow gorge was the only way to approach the landing
strip. We flew directly in for a safe landing.

Our main concern now seemed to be get to the mess hall
for something to eat, and to be assigned to our
barracks. I had to report to the office to give them my
radio log, nothing of importance on it. All routine.

That night we were outside looking at the stars. It was
the darkest sky I had ever seen, even the though it was
clear. A spectacular night with the stars very bright.
I had never been that far north

The next day we were briefed for our next flight which was Iceland, the base was Reykjavik. For the flight to Iceland the briefing officer told our pilots we would cross the icecap of Greenland, located northeast of B.W.1. base, at an altitude of 10,000 feet. An aircraft down in that area was difficult to locate. We were advised how to survive in the event of a crash on the icecap. It was dangerous crossing, some planes had been lost there.

B-17F

On Our Way to Iceland.
I was again briefed that the German submarines were jamming our radio frequencies, much the same as on the flight from Goose Bay. The communications officer advised me to monitor the radio constantly, in spite of the jamming, for any message the station wanted to send me.

We took off down the one long runway through the gorge. As we gained altitude we made a procedure turn to the right 180 degrees, to start the climb up over the icecap. It was directly ahead of us on our flight path. We suddenly ran into dense fog, visibility was zero. All the pilots could do was stay on course and hope the B-17 would climb above the cap ahead. We did not know exactly where it was in relation to us, we had no radar. We knew the icecap was at 10,000 foot altitude.

We finally broke out of the fog into clear air, the icecap below us was about 1,000 feet. The B-17 had done a great job.

As our radio navigation was being interrupted by the jamming, the navigator used the sextant to verify our position. He found he was a bit off course and made the corrections. I believe it was the only time the sextant was necessary. We were all glad we had a navigator we could rely on.

The radio static was a constant irritation to me on the entire trip, the other crew members could enjoy the ride. I do not recall if I made any contacts with Greenland except the departing procedure.

I was contacted by the station from Iceland as we were nearing that coast, perhaps 100 miles away. They instructed us to descend to below the clouds and approach the field in that manner. The clouds were about 1,000 feet above the sea, we were flying through drizzling rain.

Reykjavik, Iceland.

As instructed, we were to flying toward Reykjavik under the clouds. I had delivered the message to the pilot. Not knowing if he had received the message on his voice radio acknowledged my call.

Our landing at Reykjavik was normal. The base was another dismal looking area. The buildings were the round roofed quonset type, most were imbedded about six feet in the ground. We were told the reason being to protect them from the strong winds and blowing pumice sand. The wind seemed to blow constantly.

I do not remember seeing any vegetation, perhaps Iceland being near the Arctic Circle, winter was near. After landing and all reports were handed in. We had a brief lecture letting us know the town of Reykjavik was "off limits" to American Servicemen. Iceland was a pro-German country to a great extent.

We stayed at this base about two days. Then were briefed for the next leg of our journey, which was Stornoway, Scotland. A small city of 5,000 population. Located on the east central side of the Isle of Lewis of the Hebrides chain.

This was an uneventful flight over the sea and we landed at the small field of Stornoway. The surrounding country-side seemed old fashioned. On the edge of the runway I noticed an elderly lady with a white shall covering part of her head, much like the pictures we had seen of people in the "old countries." She was driving a cow to the barn. A wooden rail fence enclosed the lane in which she was walking.

It seemed we had regressed to a less modern day and age. I wondered if people living here knew there was a war in progress. Probably the noise of our aircraft was destroying their peace and quiet and that we may be intruders.

If one looks up the history of Scotland you find it has an early history of much political turmoil, since before the year 900. However, at this time I felt they were at peace and not engaged in this modern, or present war.

A short time before we landed here, a report of late news, reporting the war stated *"the Eighth Air Force had bombed Germany with a force of 500 heavy bombers on one mission."* We thought the war could not last long after such a massive attacks. We lived to see how very wrong we were.

Germany was much stronger than any of us had thought. Germany was well equipped and well organized. A country only a bit larger than our state of Texas. We also knew the U.S.A. was not doing their best it was capable of doing. People in the U.S.A. just did not know how serious this war could be, or what it was all about. Many did not even know where Germany was, geographically.

Landing in England.
Before we were to leave England a year later, the Eighth Air Force could bomb Germany with a force of 1,000 to 1,400 heavy bombers at one mission. This force was used repeatedly. The war was not over when I left England after completing my tour of combat flying.

Our stay now in Stornoway was overnight if I remember correctly. The final leg of our trip the next day, to Prestwick, Scotland. Only a brief stay there and we flew to the final landing of this trip, landing at Burtonwood, England. The faithful B-17 which carried us from Grand Island, we left it here at Burtonwood. We stayed overnight and left by train the next day for Stone, England for a two day stay and left there for Hemel Hempstead. Then left Hemel Hempstead for Bury St. Edmunds.

We drove through the English countryside, through one small village after another. The english children often followed the open trucks as we slowly moved through the towns. They called out, *"Hi Yanks"* and *"any gum chum?"*

Hearing this old familiar term of *"Hi Yank"* and *"any gum chum?"* I thought these same children had seen many vans and trucks carrying "replacements" such as we. Many men had preceded us along this route.

The final stop was at the 94th Bomb Group at Bury St. Edmunds. This was the group we were to fly our combat tour with. However, unknown to us at this time, "fate" would decide. We were not scheduled to be on operational status for another week or two.

Our task was now to attend orientation lectures, each crew member attended classes in their own field. I as radio operator attended radio school and was advised we would use much different operating procedures than in the "states." Using the same equipment, only procedure was changed.

How could one learn combat procedure anywhere but at a combat air base. This seemed logical reasoning.

At our group orientation lecture by the Colonel. He said, *"you men are here to fly 25 combat missions for your tour. However, at the present rate of our losses I doubt if any of you will make it through, good luck."* One could think this Colonel only knew the records of statistics, certainly he knew nothing about the "fortunes of war." No one could know that.

The statistics were, the Eighth Air Force were averaging a 5% loss on every mission. By using common arithmetic, one could figure the 5% time the 25 missions of a tour and would end up with an impossible 125% loss.

B-17G of 100th Bomb Group
350th Bomb Squadron

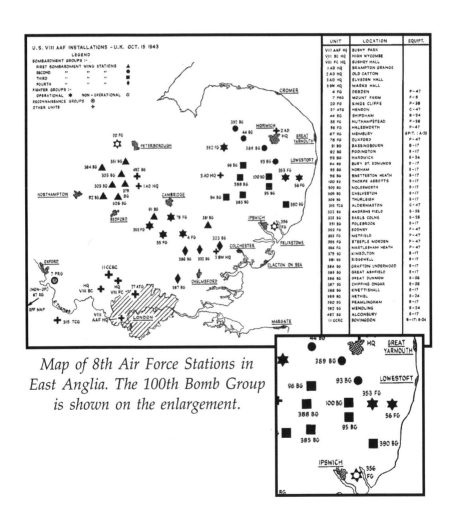

Map of 8th Air Force Stations in East Anglia. The 100th Bomb Group is shown on the enlargement.

Arriving at Thorpe Abbotts.
After talking to many active combat flyers at Bury St.
Edmunds it was easy to understand this was a rough
business. The 8th had been doing daylight bombing since
the early part of the year 1943.

We were about ready to start our operational tour at
Bury St. Edmunds when a call came from the 100th
Bomb Group at Thorpe Abbotts. They had sent out
thirteen bombers and only one returned from a mission
on October 10th 1943 and this one crash landed at the
base. The 100th Bomb Group was in need of replacements. The fortunes of war were indeed active.

Our crew was chosen to be transferred to the 100th.
We left promptly on a truck. I think we were the only
crew from this base, there may have been others, but I
do not recall. Our crew were alone in this one truck.
An officer of the 100th welcomed us as we entered the
operations office. We had been joking about arriving on
this date of October 13th. We called it a good luck omen.

When mentioning this to the officer he said *"you fellas are
listed as Crew #13 and the airplane assigned to you is #413,
also this is the 13th Air Wing."* As we were leaving he said
as an after thought. *"Oh yes, your airplane is named HARD
LUCK!* We had a good laugh at that ironic remark.

This airplane was a model B-17F. It carried us through
many missions safely. Old HARD LUCK! had flown
many combat missions prior to ours. It had set an ETO

B-17F HARD LUCK!

This is the original bomber assigned to our Crew #13. We (Crew #13) flew 14 missions in this B-17. Shown here siting on the hardstand with Ground Crew men standing in front at some date in 1943, or early 1944. HARD LUCK! was lost to enemy action in August of 1944

record for having 600 hours of flying time on the original Studebaker engines.

Our ground crew chief T/Sgt. Meyers received the Legion of Merit for his outstanding performance. We were thankful we had a dedicated ground crew. We knew our lives could depend on their skills. I continue to have much respect for skilled mechanics. We flew this airplane until we had about 17 combat missions completed, not all in this one plane.

Our crew were then selected as a Group Lead Crew and were assigned a new airplane, a model B-17G. These new planes had electronic superchargers and made formation flying easier.

The model B-17G was the latest B-17 at that time. I think actually it was the last model built. It was aluminum colored, and no interior insulation that we had in the B-17F models. A very sleek beautiful airplane.

It also had the new chin turret which carried two 50 caliber machine guns. This machine gun was mounted in the nose and was used by the bombardier. The German fighter planes were now using head on attacks, the new gun position was needed. It was a very effective new weapon for the defense of the plane.

We named this new plane "HARD LUCK! 2." We had built up some sentimental fondness for the old plane and even had faith that it would always bring us safely home. After I had left England I heard old HARD LUCK! had been shot down on her 63rd combat mission. In August of 1944.

Flying Fortress B-17F HARD LUCK!
*This B-17 was assigned to Crew #13 on October 13th 1943.
Crew #13 flew 14 missions in this B-17 prior to being issued a
new B-17G when we became a Group Lead Crew.*

Statistics of B-17 HARD LUCK!

*This Fortress was delivered to the 100th Bomb Group on the
date of August 13th 1943.*

*She flew 63 combat missions and was lost on August 14th
1944, seen going down near the city of Ludwigshafen,
Germany.*

*This B-17 set an ETO record of 600 hours with the original
engines. Engines were changed later. It had flown many hours
of non-combat flight as well.*

HARD LUCK! was well known with the 100th Bomb Group.

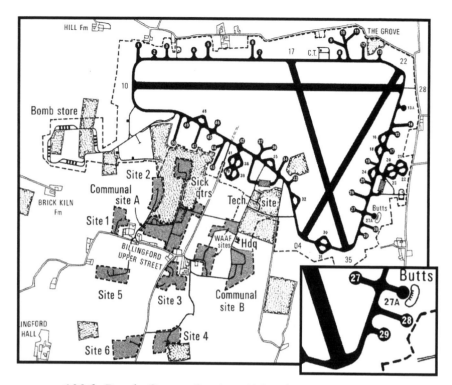

100th Bomb Group Station 139, Thorpe Abbotts,
A tiny hamlet twenty miles south of Norwich, in Norfolk
(East Anglia), England.

The size of the base map be estimated in understanding the
main runway shown at the top of the map running west to east
is a bit over a mile in length. Note the taxi strips encircling
the entire runway system, also the hardstands off the taxi strip
where the planes were parked.

The location of the hardstand 29 where we parked our plane
HARD LUCK! is noted in the enlargement in the lower right
corner of the map.

The 100th Bomb Group Control Tower...Restored
The original Control Tower of the 100th Bomb Group located at the original site. Restored to its original appearance. It is now a Historic Museum open to the public. Fully restored by the efforts of the British people, as a tribute to the 100th Bomb Group and to the flying and ground crew of that group. This was a token of the British respect extended to the 100th Bomb Group of Thorpe Abbotts, England.

As it was...1944.

Crew #13 with HARD LUCK!
Top Row L-R: T/Sgt. "Hap Holladay, S/Sgt. Bob Goodman,
S/Sgt. Jim Yarnell, S/Sgt. Clothier (took Jim's Yarnell's place),
S/Sgt. Walt Schneider, S/Sgt. Edward "Butch" Butchino,
T/Sgt. Earl Benham.

Bottom Row L-R: Lt. Jack Ogg, Capt. Loren Van Steenis,
Lt. Harold Becker, Lt. Les Torbett.

Early 8th Air Force Insignia

Experiences with Various Co-Pilots.
When we first formed as a crew, we were assigned
temporary co-pilots. During our flight training we
perhaps four different co-pilots. We finally had a co-pilot
who stayed with us and actually flew with us when we
flew our B-17 to England.

He was a Texan and wanted to fly fighter planes, We
called him "Tex" and I have trouble now recalling his
name. Just prior to us starting our combat missions, he
left. I think for B-26s. Later in the war he apparently had
returned to our base and flew again in B-17s, for how
long I do not recall. He was flying as co-pilot for a crew
of the 100th, they were forced down and taken POW.
We never have heard any more about him and have
made several inquiries.

Our permanent co-pilot on our complete combat tour
was a young Lt. Jack Ogg. He had arrived at the 100th
about the same date we did. His crew had been split up
as replacements.

Jack flew with us on all of my tour and after I had
completed my tour he had a few missions left to
complete his tour. He continued flying then as a first
pilot. While flying with our crew, he and our first pilot,
Capt. Van Steenis, had done a great job as combat pilots.
We all gave them much credit for bringing us safely back
as bad weather and formation flying was demanding of
pilots. They had to be good and no one disputes that.

We, as a crew thought our pilots were tops and we had confidence in their ability. That ability was proven many times.

Crew #13 and Ground Crew with
Aircraft #413, HARD LUCK!

Top Row L-R: T/Sgt. Glen Meyers - Crew Chief, S/Sgt. Peter Sokolosky - Mechanic, S/Sgt. Jim Yarnell - Armorer/Gunner, S/Sgt. Clothier - took Jim's place, S/Sgt. Walter Schneider - Tail Gunner, S/Sgt. Edward Butchino - Asst. Engineer, Sgt. Amos Hill - Mechanic, Sgt. Mozinski - Mechanic.

Bottom Row L-R: T/Sgt. Archie Holladay - Engineer, Lt. Jack Ogg - Co-pilot, Capt. Loren Van Steenis - Pilot, Lt. Harold Becker - Navigator, Capt. Lester Torbett - Bombardier, T/Sgt. Earl Benham - Radio Operator.

Ground Crew Mechanics with HARD LUCK!...1944.

Ground crew mechanics on the wing of HARD LUCK! at our hardstand, note the control tower in the upper left of photograph and other B-17s in the background...1944.

T/Sgt. Archie "Hap" Holladay, Flight Engineer on Crew #13 at the 350th Bomb Squadron area...1943.

Captain Loren Van Steenis, pilot of Crew #13 sitting on the nose of HARD LUCK! at the 100th...1944.

350th Bomb Squadron Insignia

S/Sgt. Jim Yarnell and Crew Chief M/Sgt. Meyers and Mechanic Sgt. Hill...1944.

Sgt. Hoffman, he gave us rides to the mess hall and to and from the plane before and after a mission...1944.

S/Sgt. John Barry, Assistant Engineer on the Devore Crew, KIA on last his mission to Brunswick 1944 and T/Sgt. Archie "Hap" Holladay, Flight Engineer on Crew #13, picture taken in front of our barracks...1943.

Bob Goodman, ball turret gunner and "Butch" Butchino, engineer of Crew #13 at the 350th Bomb Squadron area...1943.

*Earl Benham, "Butch" Butchino and "Hap" Holladay at our
barracks at the 350th Bomb Squadron area...1943.*

*Earl Benham at the
100th Bomb Group
bike parking
lot...1944.*

The 100th Bomb Group Base.

A brief description of the 100th Bomb Group base.
This field was widely dispersed, the buildings we used,
such as schools, the operations office, briefing rooms,
some equipment buildings. These were about a mile from
the barracks we used. Our mess hall about in between.

There were four squadrons, each had their own barracks
and orderly rooms. All were at different locations about
the base. We had combat crew's mess hall and ground
personnel mess hall. The reason being, our menu was
different than theirs because of high altitude flying,
certain foods were not compatible to flying.

There were three runways, criss-crossed at different
degrees of position. The one longest, was a bit over a
mile in length. A taxi strip encircled the runways.
There were what we called "hardstands" which were
attached to these taxi strips, used to park the planes on.

With widely dispersed facilities, a bicycle was almost a
necessity, we had no bus service. I bought a used bicycle
for 4 British Pounds and used it the entire time I was
there.

There were no facilities for washing clothes. The climate
was damp because of much rain. This presented a
problem for drying clothes. We were fortunate because of
two British men who would stop by and pick up our
laundry. The charges were plenty, but we did not not

haggle one bit as we appreciated this service. One of these men I knew as Mr. Pipe, the other one I never knew his name. Both men were of the "Cockney English,"their accent seemed comical to us. They seemed like nice people.

I noticed these men were not accustomed to the brash American ironic type of humor, some of the men took advantage of them. These fellows were very competitive for favors such as our cigarettes and candy we may have to give to them.

Sometimes a fellow would call out and throw a pack of cigarettes or candy which would intentionally land just out of reach of the British men. They would scramble for the package much to the delight of the one who had thrown it. Such tactics were not humorous to most if us. The two British men did not notice the insulting attitude. Not one of our crew took part in this crude form of humor.

Later, when I was preparing to leave the base for the United States, I gave my bicycle to Mr. Pipe. His son was coming home from the Navy and could use it. I have no accurate idea of Mr. Pipe's age. I think perhaps 60 years old. He would collect our laundry and his wife would wash it and he then would return it. We appreciated this service very much.

After our arrival at the 100th, we were not operational

for a couple of weeks. The 100th was almost closed down because of the heavy losses they had just prior to our arrival. I heard they could put up a few bombers and usually filled in, in some other group.

I did not know much of the technical operations of the base when we first were there. Now, as replacements, we were becoming familiar with group and were ready to be on operational status.

A Wake Up Call for our First Mission.

The day arrived when we were awakened at 2 a.m. by the squadron sergeant. I woke up as he shook my shoulder saying, *"wake up, this is it."* He knew it was our first mission and it seemed to me by his action he expected a show of apprehension from us at being called for our first flight.

I carefully did not show any concern. Our crew had been through too much to be emotional about this. This was just another day.

I believe there was some jealousy among the the ground office personnel, they thought the combat flyers were getting too much glory. I could see no glory in any of it.

Our first briefing for this mission was all new to us. This was different than practice. The briefing was as a group, then in sections. All of the crew members had special instructions.

After briefing we checked out our flying equipment,
the electric flying suits, the shoes, the "Mae Wests" and
the parachutes. All of this equipment was kept in the air
conditioned room. I had to also pick up all of the micro-
phones and headsets.

After all of us were dressed for the flight, we loaded into
open trucks for the ride out to the airplanes. On this first
flight we would not be using HARD LUCK!
Prior to all of this action we had eaten breakfast in the
cold, drafty mess hall.

Each man's duty now was to prepare his position. I had
to check the frequencies we would be using and also the
pilots radio. I had one gun in the radio room at that time
to install. It was a single flexible .50 caliber machine gun.
I had to assemble it and check it out that it would fire
when needed.

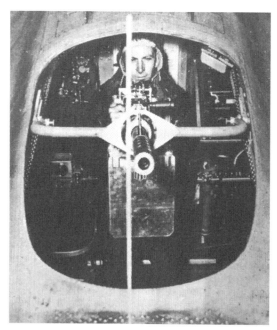

*Radio room hatch
.50 caliber
machine gun.*

Later in my tour the radio gun was removed as excess baggage. It was not located in an effective position. I was fully qualified to operate any of the gun positions if needed, all crew members were. Without effective gun defense, the airplane would be very vulnerable to the German fighter planes.

At this stage of the war, we did not have enough of our own fighter plane escort. The escort at this time was sort of a hit-or-miss schedule. The bombers had to protect themselves and defend each other.

After completing our checks and were satisfied all was in working order, we could relax in our tent at the hard stand and wait for takeoff time.

For this story now I will explain. During my combat tour I kept a diary of all of the missions I went on. I will not repeat each one here, as I will list all of my missions from my diary at the end of this story. They can be referred to as one reads this. I will refer here to the missions that were the most unusual. I will add many details about some that are not described fully in the diary.

Our First Combat Mission.
Starting with this first mission for which we had just been briefed. The one we all had worked so hard to pre-pare for and to become familiar with the routine of preparing for a mission. Now, just before takeoff time we were informed the mission had been canceled.

We returned to the operations briefing room and were told to return all of our equipment we had just drawn out a couple hours earlier. No mission credit for this effort. This was the situation we would become quite accustomed to as time went on. Many missions would be canceled after briefing and preparing the plane for flight. Many were canceled even after takeoff. No mission credit was given unless we had crossed the channel.

On November 5th, another mission scheduled. Another rush to prepare our plane for the flight. Again not our HARD LUCK! Our crew were scheduled to fly spare position. We would fill in a vacancy in event some crew aborted the mission before crossing the channel.

On this flight we took off and had a malfunction in an engine and nearly crashed into the trees at the end of the runway. Our climb to 20,000 feet was smooth enough. As we were at this altitude, I noticed my oxygen pressure was indicating very low. I knew the pilots were on the same oxygen line, so I called them. They had noticed it and we were forced to return to base as there was no way to continue without oxygen. Again no mission credit for our efforts.

On November 7th we flew our first combat mission. This was on a beautiful Sunday morning. A flight to Duren, Germany to bomb an airfield. A rather short flight of perhaps five hours flying time, we had no damage to our plane.

P-47 Fighter

P-47s

The P-47 was the first escort plane we had in the 8th Air Force. They remained as escort planes through out the war.

P-38s and P-51s were added later the famous P-47 carried the brunt of the air war. When I arrived in England, they were our main escort support. We also had aid from the British Spitfires, their flight range, not intended to to be long range, as these fighters had been designed to protect their homeland in the first part of the war. They valiantly fulfilled that job, saving their country, which allowed the American forces landing fields for the bomber.

P-38 Fighter

P-38s

The P-38 came to England to join the P-47 in escorting the bombers. At this time the P-38 had a greater range than the P-47.

This was a great fighter plane which gave the bombers much of the protection they needed. Greatly easing the strain which had been upon the P-47.

On November 16th, we had a rather spectacular target. Our second official mission. The flight I believe was a very important one to the world, so I will explain it here.

We were briefed this target was in Norway, about 60 miles west of Oslo. The name of the area was Rjukan, Norway. A hydro-electric plant which the Germans were using. 10.000 of "heavy water" in the building. A ten story structure. We were told this water was being used to help develop a powerful bomb. They said "a bomb more powerful than we could imagine."

Germany was making the atomic bomb. They were way ahead of our country on this at this time. Very few people knew anything about the atomic bomb.

The briefing for this target was: we were to fly out over the North Sea and enter Norway at an altitude of 12,000 feet and destroy the target.

The captain of the radio school asked me to remain for a special briefing after the others had left the room. He told me I would would transmit the "strike report" to England, after some of my crew members could determine the extent of the damage to the target.

After this special briefing, I was given a ride out to the plane in a special jeep. Looking very important, the crew didn't know why I was chosen to send in the strike report, I told them it was because of my skill.

The procedure was as follows:
After the crew members had given me the bombing results, I was to transmit this "strike report" to our base by Morse code. Our base would then inform the proper authorities and a photo reconnaissance airplane would go to the target site and take official photographs of the area.

The reason Captain Lash had selected me to send the report was because we were a new crew and then flying in the back of the formation, we called this position "Purple Heart Corner." I had the room to extend my "trailing wire antenna" for the the long range transmission to England.

We hit the target with a heavy concentration of bombs. The report was *"target hit and destroyed"* I saw the photos later. My transmission to England was a success, I thought as a new combat radio operator, I had done my job well, as we all had.

Our flight back to England was again over the North Sea. We were flying low over the water alone , not in formation. It was hard to realize the water under us was so cold a person would live perhaps five minutes if in the water.

We were fortunate to be riding safely above it in old

HARD LUCK! An appropriate song would have been *"nothing could be finer than to be in Carolina."* But, we were a long way from Carolina.

Some of the crew were now sitting in the radio room, their work for the flight over. I had time to remain on the radio because we were flying alone. With some luck we soon would all be safely back to base and through for the day.

Later, I was told the success of the mission delayed the German development of the atom bomb. They moved their operation into the Kiel, Germany area. This area was overrun by our invading forces, perhaps in July 1944.

Few people in the U.S.A. knew how close they were to losing the war. Why weren't they informed correctly is still a mystery to me. Do they ever think what would have happened if Germany had dropped an atomic bomb on England? Germany had the rockets to deliver it with, they did not have the atom bomb.

Perhaps the reason they did not was because of the mission we flew to Rjukan, Norway that day in November 1943.

This bombing was timed at noon when perhaps most of the people were out to lunch and hopefully away from the building that was hit. Norway and it's population were not our enemy. However, they were controlled by the Germans.

Late Fall and Winter at the 100th Bomb Group, Thorpe Abbotts, England.

Our life continued on, one mission after another. The days and nights were getting colder as winter was upon us. Our barracks was a one story rectangular flat roofed building. The walls were plastered, the exterior was a plastered stucco. The building had a capacity of 36 men.

There were three small coal and wood burning stoves which were supposed to supply the barracks with heat. One bucket of coal each day was rationed. No wood was available. The stoves were lined in the center of the barracks about 15 feet apart. This system of heating would not keep the barracks warm.

We sometimes made "raids" on the coal pile to increase our coal supply. It seemed all the buildings were cold and drafty, including the mess hall. However, that winter was not considered a cold winter, we only had one light snow that I remember.

The food at our mess hall was not great, even though we had a special menu and mess hall for the combat flyers. Flying high altitude in non-pressurized planes, many foods were not compatible. We were often without butter and the fresh eggs we were supposed to have were very few. They were supplemented with powdered eggs. which I think would have been good if prepared by experienced cooks which we seemed to lack.

Eggs were $4 a dozen on the black market. We suspected the mess hall personnel of selling our eggs. We never made a check on this proposed selling of eggs, so we had no proof.

I remember one morning we had pancakes for breakfast, we all ate too many, several of the flying men that day had gas pains in flight. A direct order was issued, "no more pancakes." To my knowledge we never had them again.

When butter was available at the mess hall, we sometimes would make a raid and take out bread and butter. We would buy a dozen eggs in trade for a carton of our cigarettes. The eggs were $4 a dozen and our cigarettes cost us 50¢ a carton. The English cigarettes cost them $4 a carton. The British were happy to make the deal and we also enjoyed the egg sandwiches we could then make in our barracks. This was a simple pleasure that made some of days more enjoyable.

When we were not flying I often was scheduled for radio school and all the other crew members were scheduled to take lessons also for their special positions, the pilots spent time in the Link trainers etc.

Our passes to London and other places were quite frequent.

We could leave the base often for the local forms of entertainment. The town of Diss was not far from our base. The lifestyle we lived was easier than the life the ground troops, who were fighting in the South Pacific or Italy or Africa were having.

There was no ground action in England by our troops at this time. The Air Force was carrying the load. Our big problem was the heavy losses of combat crews.

We met many new crews who came in as replacements, some to our barracks. One would become slightly acquainted and suddenly you realized they were gone and a new crew had taken their place.

There were three of us "old in seniority" crews, (from our barracks) We seemed to fly one mission after another and always return. Often our planes had many holes in them but would stay in the air.

These three crew were our Crew #13, (Van Steenis Crew) The "Devore Crew" and the "McClain Crew." The fortunes of war were impossible to predict or understand. Certainly a burst of devastating flak could hit a highly experienced crew as well as a new crew. Many flew quite a few missions, others would be shot down soon. Some on their first mission.

Now as I mention us three "old in seniority" crews. One of these was were shot down on their last mission to their tour. The other was lost on their 23rd mission, only two to go for completion of their tour.

This left us as the only one of the old original crews from our barracks. I will relate more about the loss of these crews later in this story. We all knew them well.

December 14th 1943, we were briefed for a mission to Berlin. We were all surprised at this because we had never been to Berlin prior to this date. We also knew at this time we didn't have enough fighter support yet to venture so far into enemy territory.

We knew the German Air Force fighter planes would be out in full force. The briefing officer said the weather was so bad over Germany their planes could not take off. We knew better.

We went out to our planes after the briefing and went through the process of getting everything ready as usual. Then the mission was canceled a few moments before takeoff. We returned to the briefing rooms and were briefed for a target at Kiel, Germany.

Again, out to the planes and prepared for takeoff. The mission was also canceled a few moments before takeoff time. No mission credit for all of this effort so early in the morning.

The security at our base was certainly tested that morning, and found to be very poor.

Some of the people living at Diss, England a short distance from our base had heard we were going to Berlin before the mission was canceled.

We were not briefed for Berlin again, that I knew of, until March of 1944. No heavy bombers of ours flew to Berlin until early March of that year.

The British RAF bombed Berlin constantly during night raids. They often used the Mosquito bomber at night. The British bombers on their way to Germany would pass over our field at night, we could hear them going over for hours, seemingly spaced at quarter mile intervals.

The German bombers often bombed cities near our area. We could see the flashes of the anti-aircraft fire high over the targets. Then the dull rumble of exploding bombs.

Christmas Eve 1943.
On December 24th of 1943, we planned we would have the day off. About 1:00 p.m. the field loud speakers announced "all combat crews report to the briefing room." This meant a mission plan in progress.

The briefing officer told us the Germans had a new rocket type weapon that carried 1,000 of TNT. This was a winged rocket, propelled by a jet engine. It did not have a pilot and was launched from a launch ramp. It would proceed in the direction it was aimed. The jet engine would carry it to the target, then would shut off and the rocket would explode on impact with a tremendous blast force.

On Christmas eve the Germans were planning a massive attack on London. The purpose was to demoralize the British population with these savage attacks.
Our orders were to stop these attacks at once by bombing their launching ramps on the coast of France. The entire 8th Air Force was alerted to take part. The British RAF also were taking part in this all out defense.

The target for the 100th was on the coast of France, we were to bomb from the almost suicide altitude of 12,000 feet. At this low altitude we were vulnerable to the German anti-aircraft fire.

We had a promise of good fighter escort, the flak was our worry. Much to our relief later, as we were over the target, the flak wasn't as bad as we had thought it would be. Some of the bomb groups had a much heavier concentration of flak at other targets along the coast. We flew back to our base in bad weather and had a rough time landing after finding the field.

The 8th lost some planes that day, none from our base. The good part being, no rocket bombs fell on London that Christmas Eve, and none for several weeks.

Later in January a few hit various places, some in London, but not on a massive scale. The British fighter planes had some time to prepare a defense against them. The rockets were much faster than a plane, so head-on attacks were the system the British used. The rockets being without pilots could not engage in evasive action, but their speed made them difficult targets.

The British action was not 100% effective, not all of the rockets were destroyed before they fell. They were a blast bomb, not fragmentation, but very dangerous, used primarily as a demoralizing weapon.

We again bombed these ramps in January of 1944. One of the missions we bombed from 20,000 feet, the flak was very heavy. We had many holes in our plane from the flak. Bombing these launching ramps was done many times in the months ahead. There were many of them along the coast line.

Later in January we heard the rocket "buzz bombs" were hitting London. The news seemed to be playing down the seriousness at the bombing.

Our flight engineer, Holladay and I were going to London on a three day leave. We were advised not to London because of these attacks. We ignored the advise and went to London.

Arriving in London, I was surprised to see so many

people again living in the underground "tubes", much the same as they had lived when the German air raids were going strong, as when I first had arrived in England. I realized now the buzz bomb attacks were more serious than we had been led to believe.

Later that night I went to a very nice hotel, located in an area where several other hotels were located around a city square. A large city park was in the center of this square, these were very nice hotels. The luxury of having a large bed with sheets to sleep on, to me was a far cry from life in our barracks.

I was awakened by gunfire about 3 a.m. I figured it was an air raid in progress somewhere in the city. I was about to go back to sleep when I heard a loud roar directly overhead, a brief pause in the noise and then the roar and vibration of a tremendous explosion. I could hear glass from the windows of the surrounding buildings falling to the streets.

I realized then that the roar I heard was the sound of the jet engine of a buzz bomb, with a near miss on my hotel. I noticed many people standing out in the hall of the hotel. I closed the door and went back to sleep.

In the morning I went out onto the street, the sidewalks were covered with broken glass, about a foot deep. The windows facing the park were mostly broken out. The bombs seemed to have landed in the center of the city park. The bandstand was mass of rubble, it had seen happier days. This blast of 1,000 pounds of TNT was devastating. Lucky that no one I heard of had been injured.

I had breakfast and went to a barbershop to get a haircut. I discussed this bombing with the barber. He said *"yes, one could land on top of my shop any moment. But I must work to support my family. If I were wealthy, I would send my family to Scotland as the wealthy people do now."*

I thought to myself, it is the poor working person who endures the worst of the war. Life was rough for the British people, a life of hardship. It was a life people living the United States could not possibly know.

I felt content I did not have to worry about my parents being bombed while I was flying combat. The German and English flyers had problems of that nature. As for me, I had little to worry about.

That day I took the train to Oxford, England. I stayed overnight at a private home. The next day, some slight sight-seeing and later went on to Norwich, later back again to the base.

After this time off, I was back into the swing of things. I noticed in the days ahead our fighter plane escort seemed better, the flak over enemy targets more intense.

January 19th 1944 the target was for installations on the

French coast. Our bomb load was 500 pound demolition bombs. Our plane had special delayed bombs in the bomb bay. We were the only plane in the group carrying this type of bomb.

The bomb had a special fuse that delayed the explosion by 24 hours after it was dropped and designed that no one could remove the fuse without it blowing up. No one knew how to remove the fuse on this special bomb. In the case of many delayed bombs, the fuse could be removed and disarm the bomb if it were found in time. This bomb was decidedly different.

The irony now was, this mission was canceled before takeoff because of bad weather. Later that day it was decided our plane would have to be unloaded.

How to get these bombs out of the plane without blowing them up? Only one solution remained and that was for us to takeoff in that bad weather and drop the bombs in a designated area in the North Sea. We were ordered to do that.

For this flight, all the barrage balloons in our flight path were to be lowered because of poor visibility. Weather was not fit to fly in. We did take takeoff with the load and went to the dropping area and dropped the bombs. I suppose the blew up 24 hours later in some unsuspecting fishes face.

Now to return to the base. On the return our navigator suddenly shouted to the pilots, *"a barrage balloon directly ahead!"* The pilots put the plane in a steep banking turn away from the dangerous balloon. I saw the balloon flash past our wing tip. A near miss that would have brought us down if the navigator and pilots had been asleep at the switch.

Not much room for error on that one. Someone had forgotten to lower this one balloon. No mission credit for this hazardous flight, just another day.

Again in January we were briefed for installations on the French coast. This time we were to bomb not by a group of 21 airplanes, but by a six plane formation. Which would make us a good target for the anti-aircraft gunners on the ground.

To make matters worse for us, we were leading this small formation. Our bombardier was the one with the bombsight. The ground gunners knew that the lead plane carried the bombsight, so if possible, we were their main target.

The bombardier had been instructed by operations to "go around again" if he couldn't find the target on the first run. In the face of all that flak, we were not eager to do that.

As we approached the target the flak was horrendous.

The bombardier saw the target and released the bombs. The pilots then put the plane in a steep bank and we got away from the area fast, and left the flak behind. Bombardier Torbett had done his job well. We landed at the base, counted several holes in the plane. A rough mission because of the flak.

Through the balance of January and February we flew several flights. Some of these flights were training flights with no mission credit toward our tour of 25.

A flight of interest occurred on February 24th 1944, a rough one to Poland. Our briefing for this flight was a German aircraft factory in Posen, Poland. This required us to fly out over the North Sea again, across Denmark and out to the Baltic Sea and then into Poland. We did not have much fighter escort at that time for this long flight. We met many German fighter planes as we continued on toward the target. Many 8th Air Force planes went down.

Weather forced us away from our target as we neared Posen, clouds forced us to an altitude 12,000 feet. We turned and went to Rostock, Germany and bombed the submarine base there. The flak was thick over Rostock. We turned toward the North Sea which was quite a long distance from us, we again met German fighter planes.

Our armorer gunner Jim Yarnell was shot through the

S/Sgt. Jim Yarnell after being grounded from wounds received on the mission on February 24th 1944, shown here with HARD LUCK! at the 100th.

shoulder and also his right hand. I heard him over the interphone when he was hit. He calmly said *"I guess they got me."* We helped him into the radio room where he could lie down. Our pilot Van, came back and gave Jim a shot of morphine to help ward off shock from a wound at high altitude. Van spent some time in the medics prior to becoming a pilot. The experience came in handy at this time.

I called the navigator and asked him how long before we would land at our base. He informed me it would be six hours as were facing a 100 mph head wind and we could not go to a lower altitude until we were over the North Sea, where the wind would not be so strong.

We were fortunate Jim had not received a more serious wound. This was bad enough. We were finally over the North Sea. We then dropped out of formation and descended to a low altitude over the sea.

We landed at our base with no further problems. The ambulance met us as we landed and took Jim to the hospital. Total flying time on this flight was 10 1/2 hours. Jim was grounded because of his injury. His flying days were over.

We were thinking, after a long mission like this our luck seemed to be with us yet. We had seen many planes go down on that mission, both German and American. Fortunately none from the 100th group.

On February 25th, the day after we had flown this long mission to Poland. We were briefed for a mission to Regensburg, Germany. We knew this would be another rough flight, because the defenses were concentrated heavily in that area.

Fortunately, on that flight we had good escort. The flak, true to our expectations, was very thick over the target. We had been informed the flak guns were mounted on top of the mountains around Regensburg giving the more altitude and closer to our formations.

We picked up several flak holes in old HARD LUCK! also one engine had been hit, it had to be shut off, or "feathered" as we called it. We came back with the three remaining engines okay. Our base was clouded up as we returned, making landing difficult. This had been a 9 1/2 hour flight.

A B-17 flying through flak on the bomb run.

After landing we were shocked to hear one of our planes was missing. It was Lt. McClain, in B-17 #788. This crew had been with us in our barracks since we first stated flying, we knew them well. They were a veteran crew, this was their 23rd mission.

The Two "Senior Crews" in our Barracks Lost.

On February 25th 1944, the target was Regensburg, Germany. The flight crew of Lt. Stewart McClain, the enlisted men of that crew lived in the same barracks as our crew. They had been there as long as we had. This day was their 23rd mission, 25 would be the complete tour.

As we approached the target, they were flying off our left wing. I saw them as we entered the flak over the target, When we emerged from the flak, they were not to be seen. I called our pilot and asked if he had seen them, he said "they perhaps picked up some flak and dropped back a bit." We never saw them again.

The story of their flight was, they lost an engine in the flak over Regensburg, they dropped back and were attacked by German fighters as they tried to returned to England alone.

The radio operator was killed by the German planes fire, many aboard were shot. As they almost reached the coast of England, they crashed into the channel. The pilots were killed as were most of the crew. The story of their flight is listed in the story "Century Bombers" on page 84. Written by one of the rescued crew members. He later returned to the United States and became a college professor. I received a letter from him in 1992 telling of this flight.

Mission to Regensburg, Formation Positions February 25th 1944.

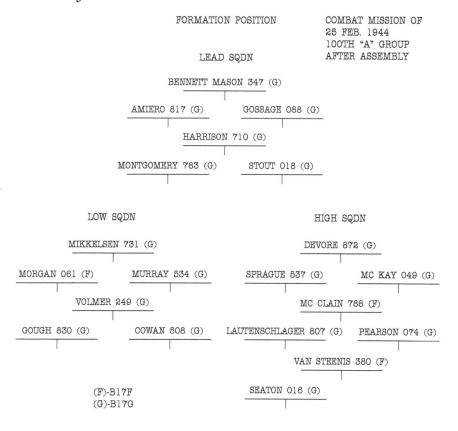

FORMATION POSITION

COMBAT MISSION OF
25 FEB. 1944
100TH "A" GROUP
AFTER ASSEMBLY

LEAD SQDN

BENNETT MASON 347 (G)

AMIERO 817 (G)   GOSSAGE 088 (G)

HARRISON 710 (G)

MONTGOMERY 783 (G)   STOUT 018 (G)

LOW SQDN   HIGH SQDN

MIKKELSEN 731 (G)   DEVORE 872 (G)

MORGAN 061 (F)   MURRAY 534 (G)   SPRAGUE 537 (G)   MC KAY 049 (G)

VOLMER 249 (G)   MC CLAIN 788 (F)

GOUGH 830 (G)   COWAN 508 (G)   LAUTENSCHLAGER 807 (G)   PEARSON 074 (G)

VAN STEENIS 380 (F)

(F)-B17F   SEATON 016 (G)
(G)-B17G

The Loss of the Second "Senior Crew from our Barracks.
This was the crew of Lt. Herbert Devore lost on their
flight to Brunswick, Germany on March 15th 1944, on
their final flight of their tour.

The enlisted crew members were living in our barracks
and had been there the entire time. This morning we
(our crew) were not scheduled to fly.

The Devore crew were elated to think this was to be
their last mission. The tail gunner, Knute Knudson was a
bit agitated because they were leading the group and
Knute had to give up his position to another man. He
was therefore "bumped" from the flight. The radio operator Harry Linke had finished his tour just previously to
this flight.

As they entered the flak over their target, they had a
direct flak hit. This forced them out of formation and as
they dropped back their airplane blew up. Only three
men survived. One was the flight engineer, Harrison
Longhi, from our barracks. He was picked up by the
Germans and was a POW until the end of the war.

Members of the "Devore Crew"

(L-R) Darrell "Cookie" Dickenson, KIA. Nickolas "Del" Del Cimmoto, KIA and Harry Link, completed tour, next to our barracks at the 100th.

S/Sgt. John Barry, Assistant Engineer, KIA.

*(L-R) Harry Linke, completed tour and
Nickolas "Del" Del Cimmoto, ball turret gunner, KIA.*

*T/Sgt. Harrison
Longhi, Flight
Engineer. He
bailed out and
became a POW.
Note the shelter in
background.*

Knute Knudson, tail gunner.

Our Nine Day Leave.

After this series of long missions we were advised, with 17 missions completed, we were eligible for a nine day leave. We called this a "flak leave." We had the option to continue flying missions to complete our tour, or we could take this leave.

Our pilot said he would leave it to a crew decision. We all voted to take this time off, our reason being the longer we could delay, the better chance we had of having more fighter protection. Van thought that a good idea, as we had heard more of the P-51s were coming to aid our faithful P-47s and P-38s.

This nine day leave passed quickly.
I did not keep a diary, so I really do not remember much about it, except I spent a good part of it in London. Some of the news we heard was not good.

T/Sgt. Earl Benham and T/Sgt. Brown on the fountain in front of the Palace in London...1944.

The 8th had started bombing Berlin while we were gone, losses were heavy. I heard one day the 8th lost 100 heavy bombers. We were lucky to be on this leave. Later, when we returned to base, we found only six men left in our barracks. Out of a full barracks of 36 men including us. There were 24 missing, just from our one barracks. They were replaced by new men, men we were not acquainted with.

Assigned as a "Group Lead" Crew.
Our crew were now notified we were selected as a "Group Lead" crew. This meant our bombardier would

carry the bombsight in the nose of our airplane. He was responsible for hitting the target. If he missed, all of the other planes would also miss as they dropped their bombs when he did.

Then the failed mission would perhaps be re-scheduled. Any plane lost then would be the result of him missing the target the first time. This was more responsibility than any young man should have to face. Yet they did face it, and in the face of deadly flak.

The lead navigator also had more responsibility, a slight error in direction and the entire mission could be jeopardized. The heavy known flak areas were listed on his map and were to be avoided whenever possible, just part of the lead navigators responsibility.

Pilots also had to work more to do, no promotions promised. We all had more work to do. I was expected to send in lead reports. The lead plane was more vulnerable to the new head on attacks of the German fighter. They knew the lead plane carried the bombsight.

The German plan of attack. The German planes would fly straight towards the formations firing 20 millimeter cannon. They flew 10 abreast, one pass could wipe out an entire squadron of bombers. Anyway, we now had the "honor" of being a lead crew. Later our pilot was promoted to captain, as was the bombardier. No one else received a promotion.

A New B-17 Named "HARD LUCK! 2."

We flew practice flights March 14th. March 15th in preparation for this lead position. These were four hour flights. On March 16th we were issued a new airplane. We named it HARD LUCK! 2. It was a B-17G model. This new G model was more adaptable for the lead plane than the older F models.

One great feature was the twin 50 caliber machine guns mounted in the nose section in a turret. This gun position was operated by the bombardier and was very effective in the defense of the airplane when German fighters made their frontal attack. It also had electronic superchargers which made formation flying easier. On March 17th, our briefing was for a target at Oberpfaffenhofen, Germany with Munich as secondary target. The target was to be an airfield about five miles north of Augsburg, Germany.

Because we were lead, we took off first. In about two hours, all formations were in position to leave the coast of England. Our altitude about 20,000 feet. As we crossed the channel and we were just over the coast of France our plane was hit by gunfire. We thought it was a German fighter using 20 millimeter shells. We never saw it, but our bombardier was hit.

The navigator in the same compartment could determine the bombardier was not conscious and notified the pilot. The pilot decided to fly perhaps five minutes to have time to assess the bombardiers condition, when flying lead it was essential that the bombardier could be in condition to accurately drop the bombs on target. The pilot soon found that the bombardier was in no condition to continue. We had to abort the mission.

The pilots procedure then was to call the deputy lead from the high squadron to take our place in the lead formation. This procedure was followed.

We then banked steeply to leave our position in the lead formation. The other planes were to hold their course and continue straight ahead. I looked out of the window and to my amazement, I saw the planes behind us following us out of formation. This was a gross error being made. The high and low squadrons were going ahead at full speed. The lead squadron, when they found their error, were too far behind to ever reform. They all headed back to England.

This was a dangerous thing to do because flying alone over enemy territory, one was vulnerable to German fighter attacks. We all made it back, our bombardier slightly wounded. His flak vest undoubtedly saved his life. Shortly after this incident he returned to flying status with us. None of the incident or error was our pilots fault. Just one of those things when someone was asleep at the wheel. After this error, we flew a couple practice flights, practicing this maneuver of leaving the lead position as we did.

Mission to Bordeaux, France.

On March 27th 1944, we led a mission to Bordeaux to bomb an airfield. This include the entire base. Looking down it was possible to see our bombs exploding on the field. Apparently a complete destructive effort.

The formation sheet shows the crews involved. This formation is a copy of an original I still have, although showing signs of age, it is a rare original.

Notice on this formation, the crew of the well known pilot McKay flew directly above and behind our lead plane, also the equally well known crew of pilot Malooly flying on our right wing.

This seems to be the value of these formation sheet, as they show crew positions in formations and recalled later when viewed by those who were there at the time. On this flight, our pilot Captain Van Steenis led the group with Major Elton, our 350th Squadron Commander as command pilot.

Mission to Bordeaux, Formation Positions
March 27th 1944.

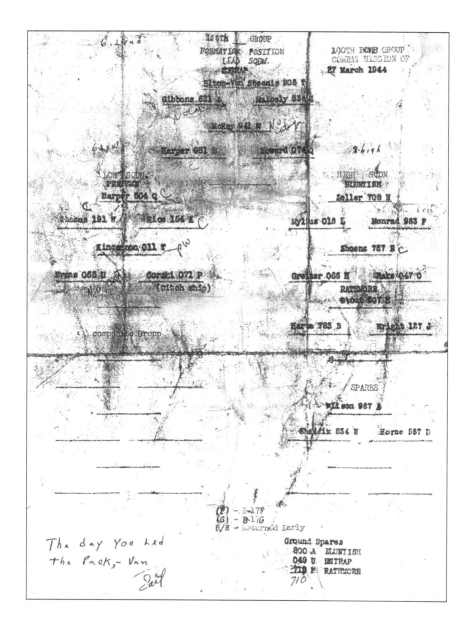

The day You Led
the Pack, - Van

P-51 Fighter

P-51s

The P-51 arrived in England with the primary purpose to escort heavy bombers to and from the targets. Their range was greater than either the P-47 or P-38.

The P-51s, the P-38 and P-47 were also used to strafe ground targets. Their performance was equal to the great fighter planes the German Air Force had.

The arrival of the P-51 gave the 8th Air Force bombers added protection from the German fighters. This aided the P-47s and P-38s which had been with us earlier in the war.

April 9th again we were briefed for Posen, Poland. After the usual preparations, we took of in very bad weather. We ran into worse weather over the North Sea.

With visibility almost at zero, it was impossible to stay in formation. We dropped out of formation and flying just above the sea we headed for England alone. When we were over the coast, we ran into more heavy rain, at our low altitude they saw an airfield that looked like we could land on it.

The pilots, with great skill, brought us safely into a smooth landing at this B-24 base, without radar, through this downpour of rain.

A field bus came out and picked us up and took us to the mess hall for a good meal. We had nothing to do until the weather cleared and we took off for home base. We landed at our base with no further problems. No mission credit for our efforts, this was just a day of fun.

April 11th, after a day of comparative rest, we were again briefed for Posen. The weather again was bad as we took off at 7 a.m. and climbed to altitude out over the North Sea. Weather making it almost impossible to keep a good formation.

Many of our planes became lost in the clouds and returned to England, This made our group ragged and weak as we crossed the coast of Denmark. We wanted a strong formation as our group was positioned on the outside of the entire wing formation. We knew the Germans would be out in force and would attack the weaker side. Our 100th Bomb Group was in a vulnerable position.

When we were nearing the Baltic area, I looked out of the radio room and saw to the right and about 5,000 feet above us, what looked a flock of black birds that we used to see on the farm back in Minnesota. I knew these were German fighter planes waiting for the signal to attack. I estimated there were 200 or more of them.

We watched them string out in a long line and pull out ahead of us. Then they turned towards our formations and made their attack. At their first pass I saw some B-17s go down into the Baltic Sea, as well as some fighters. I could see the wakes of the rescue boats out to pick up survivors. Many parachutes visible for brief moments.

This battle was not easy for either the bombers or the German fighters as each had to face the tremendous fire power pitted against them. Not a pretty picture. Fortunately at the speed of it all, the battle may have lasted 10 minutes at it's most severe attack.

We at high altitude may have been at 300 mph and the German fighters a bit faster. A few moments seemed a long time. This attack ended as fast as it started and we were still on our way to Posen. Many bombers had been lost.

As we neared Posen, the clouds were so thick they made visual bombing impossible. We were forced to turn and again strike Rostock, Germany We encountered very heavy flak over Rostock.

After this strike, we again headed toward the North Sea and the long trip over water to our base at Thorpe Abbotts. On the way to the coast, we were again attacked by German fighters.

These attacks were not as heavy as previous ones have been. I expected our escort at the coast had been active and had dispersed many of them.

We had a lot of respect for our fighter pilots and we respected the German fighter pilots as well. The German flyers were fighting for their country, right or wrong, as we were. I felt no hatred for the German pilots.

We made the long flight over the North Sea to our base and landed safely once again. This had been another 10 1/2 hour flight, very similar to the flight on which Jim Yarnell was wounded.

On this flight to Posen we were using our new B-17G which had the twin .50 caliber guns mounted in the nose of the plane, in what we called a "chin turret." This gave the bombardier some real firepower. Very effective weapons to guard against the head-on attacks by German planes.

The older planes a was HARD LUCK! did not have these chin turrets. They had instead only a single .50 caliber

The B-17G with the chin turret.

machine gun, which was used by the bombardier. On our new airplane, the radio gun was removed because it had an ineffective location. It had very little mobility and could only be fired effectively when enemy planes flew directly overhead. When in our old plane, I had fired it only once at an enemy plane.

We were attacked at that time by JU-88s, they were heavily armored on their underside and would make attacks from the side and fly directly overhead and make a steep banking turn off to the left. As this one flashed overhead, I shot perhaps 20 rounds. I thought I saw my shells hit the underside and explode, but perhaps harmlessly on the armor plate.

On that day we were attacked a few times by these JU-88s with their .30 caliber and 20 millimeter shells. We had also encountered some flak.

The usual event after we landed was to examine the plane for bullet holes and assess the damage. As we were doing this we saw a 20 millimeter shell hole about two feet above our tail gunners position, through the rudder stabilizer, not too far from the tail gunners head.

Tail gunner Walter Schneider had been with us since Moses Lake, Washington. If this shell had exploded as it was intended, it perhaps would have killed Walt and possibly torn off our tail.

We all laughed at Walt's facial expression when he saw how close this shell had been to him. I also had a flak hole above the window in the radio room, right beside my desk. Sitting at the desk, I could look through the hole. I found the piece of flak, embedded in the metal of the plane. I carried it in my pocket for years, but finally lost it.

It seemed we were using up our luck on these so called "fortunes of war episodes." We had returned from so many near misses, how much longer would it last? No one knew and did not care to speculate.

I had heard after these three months we had of operational

flying, there were only three of the sixteen crews left. The crews we had flown overseas with, as the provisional replacement group. Our crew was one of the remaining three. About this time I am sure we were thinking, *"all for what?"* But our morale remained high.

The next few pages of this story I will remark about some very unusual events that occurred. These events are all true events, the dates are not certain in many cases. Only some that pertain to missions may be dated.

Trips to London.
We started on our way to London from our base by taking the field bus to the station at Diss. Diss was a small town about 2 miles from our base. Arriving at the station we noticed it was a small, rather antique looking brick building, one had the sense of Old England in each and every brick.

The cost of fare to London was very moderate. The distance to London was near 95 miles, which took about two and a half hours of jostling along the rails. The high pitched whistle of the engine was a strange sound to us who were accustomed to our American locomotives.

Usually there were several men from our base on the train who we were acquainted with. So the trip was spent in conversations and the usual banter of comrades.

It was a pleasure to watch the landscape of England

pass by the train car windows, beautiful and quaint. We had seen it many times from the B-17s as we flew over, however, the nearness of the scenes were enjoyable and relaxing. Relaxing, while trying to push the thoughts of the war from our mind. Usually the "London leave" consisted of three whole days. to live and enjoy.

When entering the huge station in London, one was first impressed at the scenes of destruction of war to the city. The effort of getting a cab or going to a hotel was one of the first efforts to be considered. There were times when we left the task if finding a hotel until later in the evening.

Faced with the attraction of the many historical sights available in London, a stranger had to make the effort to see some of it at least.

To actually stand looking out the window of the Tower of London, the very window Sir Walter Raleigh had looked from, as well as many other people from the far distant past, was unusual and a great experience.

Much ancient history, I suppose we didn't appreciate it all as well as we should have. Now today, we can feel some regret that we didn't as we may look back in retrospect to that time of 50 years ago.

St. Paul's Cathedral was a great historical sight, it was heavily damaged at that time by the air raids. The first time I heard the chimes of Big Ben, I was walking across the nearby bridge. I recognized the sound at once, as we had heard the chimes in movies or radio programs. Many of these sights and sounds from this ancient city of London were very impressive to us young Americans.

We were young people who thought of the futility of war. Thoughts also, that we now were observing these ancient buildings which had withstood a thousand years of existence prior to our visiting. Thoughts also, would man in his greed and stupidity, demolish these ancient structures in the madness of war?

Later as darkness of night crept over the city, the first signs of a "blackout" made us fully aware of the dangers of the air raids that hit the city repeatedly, with disastrous results to the people. The "blackouts" were one of their defenses.

The damage we had seen now was only a small portion of the damage to the lives of the valiant British citizens. They had endured many air raids during the war.

Finding a cafe where we could get a good dinner was somewhat of a problem. The British had a strict food ration system in force. This did not allow a wide selection food at these cafes. Some black market operations were in action.

We often attended restaurants that in the past had perhaps quite a stylish atmosphere, however, now they only had nice table settings and professional waiters who could not offer a diversified menu to which they had been accustomed. Being a professional waiter, carried a degree of dignity and to support this dignity was rather rough under the circumstances.

Walking the streets of London during the blackout was another experience worth mentioning here. By comparison today when we say *"don't walk the streets unless under good lighting."* While here in London, walking in the darkened streets was necessary. The only lights permitted, were very small, dim light over the door of a business place, usually a bar or cafe. Then as one entered the door, you came first to dimly lit small room which led into the lighted area of the interior.

Walking about in the dark street one often was contacted by a "lady of the evening" who would first feel of your arm which may reveal your military rank. They well knew the higher the rank, usually the more money you may have to spend. They wanted to make money, or at least have a good time. The street noises often would echo and re-echo with the laughter and voices of many people walking the streets.

To the people who were not accustomed to this, it was very exciting the first few times one was faced with situation. Eventually after a few visits one became accustomed to this way of life and accepted it and seemed to know your way around in spite of the darkness.

London is one of the first cities to build a system of underground transportation railways, that were called "tubes" because the trains traveled through these underground tubes. These "tube" stations were a haven of protection for people who had no other air raid shelter.

The way the tubes were constructed, a brief explanation here. From the streets one would go down a series of steps to the lobby or area called a station. The trains stopped in this area and passengers either got off or on at that place.

This open area, or station is where the people seeking protection from air raids would live. The accommodations were crude, especially for those with small children. However this was one of the many trials the British people faced, with much courage.

Visiting Norwich, England.
Norwich in the year of 1943, a city of 20,000 population. The city had been bombed several times by the German Air Force. It is a historical city and carries a long history of British events.

Visiting Norwich for the first time, one could see the bomb damage. From a low flying airplane, one could also see the city was ringed by bomb craters that had missed their targets and fell to the ground on the outward side of the city. No doubt some farm homes had been hit in some instances by these bombs.

Norwich was about twenty miles for the 100th Bomb Group at Thorpe Abbotts. My first experience to Norwich was one late afternoon, as our Crew #13s flight engineer, T/Sgt. Holladay and I were returning from London and did not have to report to the 100th base until noon the following day.

I made my decision to go to Norwich instead of returning to the base at this time. I arrived at Norwich as night was falling, during a drizzling rain, this added to th darkness. The city of Norwich also was under "blackout" rules. As I left the train and started walking toward the city, I walked across a bridge that was near the station. Noticing a canteen or restaurant near by. I entered and noticed quite a crowd of people sitting at plank style tables. The thought of having a light lunch and coffee appealed to me.

I sat sat down and was enjoying my lunch and started conversation with some of the people sitting near by. Most were British soldiers of the Royal Engineering Corps. I realized the night was late, or rather it was early in the morning, as I left this restaurant.

When I started walking to the city it was raining, so I

returned to the railroad station and boarded a train that was on the way back to Diss and the 100th Bomb Group base.

This had been my first contact with Norwich. Several times later, I did see much more of the city. Many years later, I have had conversations with people from England who are living in Norwich and have walked across this very bridge I first walked across from the railroad station that rainy night, so long ago.

Goodman's Close Call...and Butch Lost his Boots.
We had an anxious incident on a mission one day, while flying at an altitude of 25,000 feet. At these higher than normal flights, the danger of an oxygen shortage to a crew member was always present.

On these occasions, our bombardier was designated to make frequent oxygen check calls to each crew position. This was done over the planes interphone system and his calls would be acknowledged by the man in that position.

When he called the ball turret gunner, there was no answer from S/Sgt. Bob Goodman in the turret. The ball turret was silent! The two men in that section of the plane manually rotated the ball turret to enable them to open the door of the turret.

They saw Goodman slumped over his controls, unconscious.

I hooked up a walk around bottle of oxygen and walked back to the turret. I saw Goodmans face and his skin was a blue color, indicating he was completely out of oxygen. We thought he had gone to the great beyond.

We plugged his oxygen hose that was dangling from the oxygen mask on his face, into an oxygen bottle, turned it to full rich mixture. To our happy amazement, Goodman revived and was in good shape. Had the bombardiers check call been as little as two minutes later, this ending would have been tragic. This was just another "near miss." Such were the "fortunes of war."

Another incident which could have been tragic, however turned out great. Our engineer, S/Sgt. "Butch" Butchino was at his waist gun position when a 20 millimeter shell entered his area through the bottom of the plane. It exploded with tremendous force, knocking Butch over backward. As he looked up he saw a fragment of wool in the air. He thought, *"are those my own flying boots?"* He felt no pain and seemed okay.

After a few seconds, he saw the shell had entered his flight bag which had been positioned on the floor near where he had stood. The contents of the bag had absorbed the shrapnel from the 20 millimeter shell. Butch was unharmed! Again, the "fortunes of war" were very evident.

Butch Butchino & Jim Yarnell.

Another incident of extra interest. As we were coming home across the channel from a mission, we had two incendiary bombs hanging up in the bomb bay. They would make landing hazardous, so they had to be removed by dropping them in the channel.

S/Sgt. Butchino and S/Sgt. Jim Yarnell were called to the rescue. As they were working to loosen the bombs, I happened to open the radio room door which opened into the bomb bay. I saw these two men standing, straddling the open bomb bay door, nothing under them but the English Channel, about 5,000 feet below.

They were working without parachutes on, as the small area was too close for the bulky parachutes. They loosened the dangerous bombs and the bombs fell out harmlessly into the channel. They had completed the job.

These two crew members had risked their lives that the plane now could land safely. Such were the men on crew #13, and why we we developed much respect for them.

Chaff.

One day I had some time to spend leisurely. I rode my bike out to our airplane. When I arrived, I noticed some men working on the window of the radio room. They were removing the window right beside my desk.

I remember I wasn't too happy about that, as they were covering it with a piece of sheet metal.

This metal had a chute attached, with a small cover attached to the chute which would shut from within the radio room. All this was obstructing my view out the window. The big question that no one seemed to answer was, "what was going on?" I found the answer shortly at briefing.

The German anti-aircraft guns relied on some radar to detect the bombers altitude when we were flying above the clouds. They used radar to determine our positions. Someone had thought of the bright idea of frustrating their radar by having bombers drop small strips of paper with a metal coating on one side. Their radar would pick this up and a false reading to the ground guns, as the paper slips slowly drifted down.

Naturally, the first bombers over the target received no benefit from the paper. The first time we used it, we were Bombing Hamm, Germany. The flak was horrendous for us as we went over the target. The paper was bundled in small packets about a foot long and two inches square.

They could easily be slid out of this window chute in the radio room. My duty as we were going over the target area was to put this paper through the chute. It would scatter when it hit the slipstream and fall to the ground.

I enjoyed this task because when flying through the flak over a target, there was nothing to do but sit and listen to the deadly explosions. This gave me something to do to keep my mind off the flak. All of the planes in our group were dropping this "chaff."

As we we pulled away from the target about ten miles, I could look back and see the other group making their bomb run through the same area we had been. I noticed the flak was bursting about 500 to 1,000 feet below them. The ground guns were completely fooled and were shooting at the metal strips we had dropped.

This chaff would only be useful when we were above the clouds. At least it worked for a while. Just one of the many little events of aerial warfare.

After we had landed that day. S/Sgt. Walter Schneider said *"this may be great, but it certainly didn't help us today."* We had several holes in our plane from the flak we had encountered. Walt was right, it hadn't helped us at all, but it did help the groups behind us a bit later.

We used chaff many times. I never found if it was very effective. However, we used to say *"the rougher the flak, the faster we threw the chaff."*

Crash of Three Airplanes on the Runway.
There were times when in my free time, I would go out to the flight line, usually where our plane was parked

and watched the returning bombers as they were landing from a mission. Some of the landings were quite spectacular. There were incidents of planes landing with only two engines or worse.

One day I saw three B-17s crash into each other at the end of the runway. I will comment on this one because there were no injuries.

The landing conditions that day required the use of the shorter runway. The first B-17 landed long on the runway, he had trouble getting stopped before he came to the end of the runway. He slid sideways and sort of ground looped.

The next plane coming in behind the first one also landed long and couldn't stop in time to avoid a collision with the one already crashed. Then the third plane coming in thought he had made it, however he slid into the other two that had crashed.

There were three B-17s in a pile of wreckage. As the damage was assessed, they found all three were completely ruined. Fortunately and miraculously, there were no injuries. I remember we said jokingly, *"send us $900,000 worth of war bonds to pay for these three airplanes."*

Another spectacular crash that was a total loss, and again no one injured. Two pilots, I believe were taking a

B-17 out to slow-time an engine. Somehow two flight nurses went along for the ride.

The flight was illegal as they did not have an engineer or radio operator aboard and I think no tower clearance. There were only the two pilots and the two flight nurses aboard.

As they started their takeoff run, they gained flying speed and lifted off, then lost control of the plane after the wheels were retracted. The plane came down and slid across the field, it went off the airfield and slid between two trees that fortunately tore off both wings and the gas tanks.

This left only the bare fuselage of the plane. It continued to slide forward for perhaps a fourth of a mile until it crashed into a farmers small brick barn. The story said the farmer was in the barn milking. However, the impact pushed the long nose of the B-17 way back flush with the windshield. The airplane was a total loss. No one could figure how anyone in the plane could have survived. They were all okay.

If this was an error, it was taken lightly. We needed good pilots to fly missions and these were good men, in spite of their deviation from the rules and regulations that day.

The incidents of this story may be slightly different than told here, as I did not witness this crash, I have heard a few different versions, however basically it is authentic.

The IFF Switch.

We often carried a camera on our B-17 mounted underneath the airplane. This was a professional camera mounted by the office of photography for the purpose of getting pictures of the French coastal areas as we passed over. This gave our Intelligence Department evaluations of German ground movements and operations.

My duty with this venture, was to turn on the camera at the right time. I was the "official photographer." My sole duty was to "flip the switch."

Another "switch" duty I had was to activate our "IFF" (identification, friend or foe). This was a high frequency transmitter which sent out an automatic signal to the ground station.

The signal would identify us as a friendly aircraft approaching the English Coast alone. We were instructed to be at, or above 1,000 feet altitude when entering England from the channel. We were subjected to British coastal gunfire if these requirements were not met. The "switch" in this situation was more important than the one with the camera.

I will relate one incident in relation to this condition.

We were returning from a mission alone, and had descended to about 100 feet above the water of the English Channel. It was fun to fly at 170 mph at that low altitude over the water. We thought that was fast at that time in history.

As we were approaching the coast, I suddenly noticed we were nearing the White Cliffs of Dover, or the English coast line. I turned on my IFF and thought we were too low to clear the coast at the required 1,000 feet. I called the pilot on the interphone and said "remember the 1,000 foot rule." He said "well lets do it now" and he pulled up steeply.

The White Cliffs of Dover flashed under our wings, a very spectacular sight, and we were over the 1,000 foot level. The rapid climb was a thrilling ride, one wished for a camera to take a picture. Possibly our pilot had planned it that way. I am sure he had not forgotten the 1,000 foot regulation. Pilot Van was a man who loved to fly and made our flights spectacular whenever possible. He was one of the best pilots.

A P-38 Crash in Bad Weather.
One day when weather was not fit to fly in, we were all grounded with our various tasks, perhaps attending a lecture or going to our individual classes for an hour or so. But mostly doing nothing. It was a day of relaxation. A dreary drizzly day and not over 300 foot ceiling at best. Not a day to be flying.

I was lying on my bunk later in the day as were several others, reading or dozing. A loud roar of a low flying aircraft went right over our barracks. After a short pause we heard a loud explosion. I looked out of the barracks window and much to my surprise, I saw a man floating down out of the low clouds with a parachute, very near our barracks.

We all went out as he landed nearby We saw this young man, a P-38 pilot. He had passed over our area and pulled into the overcast and the plane probably going 300 mph. For a fraction of a moment, he said he had lost all continuity. He didn't know if he was right side up, going up or down. He hit the ejection button. The P-38 made a loop and went straight into the soft ground.

We found the area where it had hit, it was buried deep into the ground. The explosion had cleared an area of about 500 feet in diameter. Just a few pieces of the planes fuselage scattered about. No mechanical parts visible.

The P-38 was quite a large plane with two engines and a tricycle landing gear. Strange to think it all had disappeared into the ground.

This was one very lucky young man. He didn't have much time to decide to leave the aircraft. To the best of my knowledge, we never heard any more about this accident, or who the pilot was. I guess we had more important things to think of. This incident was just the run of the mill, just another day.

There were many of these incidents, just too many to write about. Some were serious and others comical and enjoyable. Such as the time we, just our plane, was returning from a single non-combat flight in England. As we were on final approach, flaps down, the engines purring gently, about ready to touch down. I had my papers all gathered up ready for the landing.

The engines suddenly roared to full power and we raced along about five feet over the runway, then the climbing turn at the end of the runway. We proceeded then to make a normal landing.

After we had landed, I asked the pilot what happened. He said *"as we were coming in the first time, I saw a British man riding his bicycle down the runway and I just had to make him get off his bike."* We had a good laugh about that.

I told the pilot *"we were quite low."* He answered, *"no, I still had a foot to go before the props hit the ground."* We no doubt owe this English gentleman an apology.

An Incident with a JU-88.
One early morning we were in our barracks, a dark grey day, flying conditions were questionable. We heard

and felt a loud explosion. We also heard some machine gun fire.

Everyone in our barracks made a mad dash for the brick slit trench we had outside our barracks. Butch and I stopped to put on our shoes and found we were the last ones into the trench, (we thought we were fast!) Some of the men were wearing only underwear and no shoes, standing in the cold, wet trench.

What really happened was, because of the bad weather the intended mission for that day was to be led by a Pathfinder plane. This special plane was a B-17 equipped with devices that allowed it to drop bombs on a target from above the clouds. This plane was hangered at different field than ours.

As it was to lead our group that morning, it flew in and as it approached our field , the traffic lights of the field were turned on for a moment. A German JU-88 followed it as it approached our field. Just as it was landing, the JU-88 fired at it. plus dropping two 500 pound bombs on our runway.

That was the explosion we had heard, we were perhaps a mile away. This blew a hole directly in the intersection of our two runways. A hole about 30 feet in diameter and about 10 feet deep. We had intended to use those runways that morning.

No damage had occurred to the Pathfinder that landed and the German plane was not shot down. Our mission was delayed about an hour while the runway was repaired. This repaired section remained rough for quite a few days, we would be almost at flying speed when we would cross the spot. The plane would balloon up a bit and settle back down on the runway until takeoff speed was reached.

With a full load of gas and bombs, we weren't to happy about this bounce. I assume, even to this date, many who were involved with the 100th Bomb Group base remember this bump on the runway.

An Event in Bad Weather.
On this mission we were scheduled to fly spare, our plane developed a runaway supercharger at takeoff. The pilots had to feather the one propeller and complete the takeoff with the three engines. We had 2,700 gallons of gas and a full load of incendiary bombs.

The day was cloudy with a light rain falling, visibility almost zero, a 300 foot ceiling. Many other planes in the air at the time. Our pilots knew we had to make an emergency landing.

On the first attempt, they could not line up properly because of poor visibility. We were about 20 feet above the runway, I looked out the radio room window and saw the Englishmen working on the runway, scatter in all directions. They thought we were going to crash. Pilots, Jack and Van made the proper moves and landed us safely on the second attempt.

We parked the plane and were transferred to another plane and again took off in the bad weather. We followed the formation out to the designated place over the North Sea. No one had left the formation, we as spares had no place to fill in. We returned to base and again landed with a full load of bombs in bad weather. No mission credit, just another day of fun.

A Radio Event.
Our radios during the war operated on low frequencies. Frequencies often were in the hundreds of K.C. range. Even the distress signal was only 500 K.C. Cycles today are called "hertz." These low frequencies were subject to many interruptions and interferences. It was the best we had at the time.

The directional, or navigational services for radio were good in England. A radio operator could receive direct headings to the desired landing area, also weather reports for the landing site. These reports were necessary in bad weather which was common in England.

The radio operators "QDM" could guide the airplane directly over the field. No provisions were made for the pilot to find a certain runway, as we had no radar.

These low frequencies had a short range on voice. We used carrier wave or C.W. Using the international Morse code for longer range transmissions. Voice was usually not over 50 mile range One characteristic of the low frequencies was what we called a "skip wave" and "ground wave." These terms are a simple explanation.

However, the ground wave was a direct signal from the plane to the station and vise versa. The skip wave would bounce from the ground up to the ionosphere, or heavyside layer of our atmosphere high above us and then return to earth.

This left a gap in the transmission in the area as the signal wave jumped to and from the ionosphere. We called this a "dead spot" as no transmission could be heard in that area. This area would change location from hour to hour as the ionosphere would rise and fall because of temperature changes of day.

This made it impossible to accurately determine where the gap in transmission would be. When we reached this gap we relied on the airplane to fly out of it, usually an a few moments.

On one occasion we we had been flying a lead mission and had the Squadron Major flying with us as Command pilot. As we were coming back, about 100 miles away from our base, *note, too far for voice transmission.* The major called me on the interphone and asked for a weather report at our field. I tried and found we were in a "skip wave area" or dead spot. I recalled the major and told him "you will have to wait a moment for the weather report." His answer was gruff, saying " *I didn't ask in a few moments. I want it now.*" I answered *"you'll have to wait."*

After we landed our navigator jokingly said to me *"you should use more military courtesy to a major, "sorry sir, etc."* I had to laugh when I thought of it. I should have said *"sorry sir."* That was military courtesy that we never used.

We probably did have a decided lack of formal military courtesy. Our own officers were more concerned that each man completed his duty well. We just thought nothing more was required. I had done my job well.

Tour Increased to 30 Missions by General Doolittle.
In February of 1944, General Jimmy Doolittle had increased the combat tour to 30 missions instead of the original 25. We, our crew, were extended to 28 missions on a pro-rated basis because we had 17 missions completed, we were exempt from the 30 mission order.

We thought, ironically enough, his reasoning for the extending the tour was that now, as fighter support was becoming better, some crews may live through the original 25 missions.

At least that is what we thought of the general's orders. He perhaps had other reasons. Most certainly many crews would be lost flying 30 missions that would have been completed had they flown the original 25.

General Doolittle never explained this decision. I could never understand the importance of it. There was no shortage of flying crews, that I knew of. This seemed an illogical order.

Mission With a 1,000 Pound Bomb Under Each Wing.
On April 20th 1944, our briefing was to bomb again the rocket installations on the French coast. I think these targets were the heavily armored gun emplacements. We were to bomb in a six plane formation over the target. This was a very dangerous flight, our crew would again lead this formation.

Our plane, and only ours, had a 1,000 bomb mounted under each wing. The two 1,000 pounders, plus ten 500 pound bombs in the bomb bay made quite a load.

We had never carried 1,000 pound bombs under the wing before. This procedure had never been used prior to this mission. It had been tested by the Assistant Group Lt. Colonel Kidd. This Colonel Kidd was a respected pilot and would not ask anyone to do something he wouldn't do himself.

However, we were the first to use it under enemy gunfire.

We had to face the possibility that a bomb shackle could be damaged by flak before the bomb was dropped. If the bomb could not be released and dangling under the wing, a safe landing would not be possible, we would then have to bail out.

We did not know the plane could takeoff with the big load as the Colonel had proven, this was an experiment and we did not like it at all.

After a normal takeoff, we climbed to altitude and approached the French coast. We started to draw their coastal gunfire. The pilots could do some evasive action and we weren't too concerned about the coastal flak. We were thinking of the heavy flak over the target when the bombardier had to hold the plane steady and level for an accurate bomb run.

By the time we were on the bomb run and almost to the drop point, the flak was horrendous. Above the roar of the plane we could hear the dull thud of the exploding flak shells near our plane. The explosions sounding loud and ominous.

We all knew any one of the rather innocent looking puffs of black smoke, carried with it a tremendous blast force and shrapnel, that could blow us out of the sky with one burst.

When the bombardier released the bombs, the plane

lurched a bit as one of the 1,000 pound bombs under the wing delayed a fraction of a second, then we were free and clear!

The pilots put the plane in a steep banking turn and we left the flak behind. We made an uneventful flight back to base. After landing we found several flak holes in our airplane.

We could hope this bombing had helped destroy the heavy gun emplacements the Germans were planning to use to deter the ground forces if the Americans should try to invade the coast.

This was all before the D-Day invasion. These gun emplacements were so heavily armored, perhaps our bombs had done very little damage.

A Group Lead Mission.
April 22nd 1944, we were briefed to lead the group again. This time was to be a trip to Hamm, Germany. Bombing altitude of 23,000 feet. Our bomb load was ten 500 pound bombs.

We were leading most of the 8th Air Force that day. We had the Group Colonel with us. Colonel Kelly was on his first mission with the group, now only as an observer in our plane. We also had our Squadron Commander Major Elton riding as command pilot with us.

Our co-pilot rode in the tail section, this bumped S/Sgt. Walter Schneider off the flight. Our co-pilot Jack Ogg was the co-pilot we had since arriving at the 100th. He was a young man of 21.

The fact that Walt missed this flight put him one mission behind our flight engineer Holladay and myself. This almost cost Walt his life in a later mission. He would have finished when I and Holladay did. Our pilot also was one mission behind me. The rest of the crew had missed some missions.

I will write later in this story about Walt and Van's tragic last mission.

On this lead flight to Hamm, we were out in front of most of the 8th Air Force. Hundreds of bombers behind us. It was a sight that would never be duplicated in the years ahead.

There were no special problems on this flight, our fighter escort was good. The German fighters did not bother us. The flak over the target of Hamm was extremely heavy, although I didn't hear of anyone in our group being seriously hit.

We had taken off at 3 p.m. and landed at 9:30 p.m. A 6 1/2 hour flight. Our navigator had performed a super job of navigating this mission. I think he received a special commendation for his outstanding efforts.

Colonel Kelly who was with us had recently been assigned as Group Colonel to the 100th and this was his first time on a combat flight, flying with us as an observer. Tragically, a week later Colonel Kelly was killed on a mission over the coast of France, as were most of the lead crew he was flying with, while bombing a rocket ramp installation.

Mission to Hamm, Formation Positions April 22th 1944.

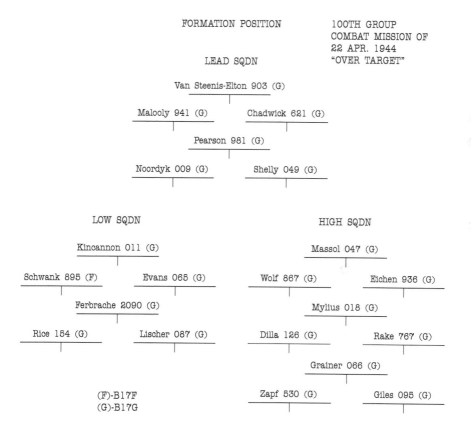

FORMATION POSITION

100TH GROUP
COMBAT MISSION OF
22 APR. 1944

LEAD SQDN

"OVER TARGET"

Van Steenis-Elton 903 (G)

Malooly 941 (G)   Chadwick 621 (G)

Pearson 981 (G)

Noordyk 009 (G)   Shelly 049 (G)

LOW SQDN

HIGH SQDN

Kincannon 011 (G)

Massol 047 (G)

Schwank 895 (F)   Evans 065 (G)

Wolf 867 (G)   Eichen 936 (G)

Ferbrache 2090 (G)

Mylius 018 (G)

Rice 154 (G)   Lischer 087 (G)

Dilla 126 (G)   Rake 767 (G)

Grainer 066 (G)

(F)-B17F
(G)-B17G

Zapf 530 (G)   Giles 095 (G)

Mission to Hamm, Route as Briefed
April 22th 1944.

Mission to Hamm, Lead Navigator's Narrative for Lead Mission of April 22nd 1944.

HEADQUARTERS
ONE HUNDREDTH BOMBARDMENT GROUP (H), AAF
Office Of The Operations Officer
APO # 559

23 April 1944

SUBJECT: Lead Navigator's Narrative For Mission Of 22 April 1944.

TO   : Commanding Officer, 100th Bombardment Group (H), Army Air Forces.

1. The 100th group led the 13 B Combat Wing behind the 13 A Combat Wing to the target. After bombs away the 100th group led all the combat wings out.

2. Route Flown: At 1731 hours we were over Manningtree and met both high and low groups. At 1735 hours we were 8 miles left of Buncher #22. We were 5 miles right of Buncher #12 at 1739 hours in division formation behind the 13 A Combat Wing. We passed over Buncher #9 on time and left the coast 2 miles left of course near Lowestoft at 1753 hours, one minute behind time. We reached the enemy coast on course 52 36 N, 04 37 E at 1819 hours, one minute late. We crossed the Zuider Zee at 52 23 N, 05 45 E on time and proceeded to 52 03 N, 06 20 E at 1835 hours, one minute behind time. At 1842 hours we turned south to I.P. but couldn't see it. We saw the target at 1850 hours and turned to it using 51 43 N, 07 25 E as our I.P. The I.P. which we used was five miles SE of briefed course. Bombs were away at 1855 hours in target area. We turned right to a point 51 40 N, 08 00 E at 1859 hours. The combat wing which was designated as lead was to the right and behind so we led out. Pilotage point at 1918 hours of 50 32 N, 07 19 E on briefed course. At 1935 hours we were 3 miles south of briefed course at 50 28 N, 06 30 E. At 1955 hours we were at 50 30 N, 05 07 E, two miles south of briefed course. We crossed the enemy coast out on briefed course 51 18 N, 02 41 E at 2035 hours.

3. We used arbitrary I.P. after failure to find briefed one but we were able to see the target. I.P. was 51 43 N, 07 25 E at 1851 hours. The flare signal was given and doors opened. The bomb run was very short and bombs fell about 300 yards short in the city.

4. Navigational instruments functioned well.

5. Difficulties: The only trouble we had was finding the I.P.

HAROLD C. BECKER,
1st Lt., Air Corps,
Lead Navigator.

Mission to Hamm, Lead Bombardier's Narrative for Lead Mission of April 22nd 1944.

HEADQUARTERS
ONE HUNDREDTH BOMBARDMENT GROUP (H), AAF
Office Of The Operations Officer
APO # 559

23 April 1944

SUBJECT: Lead Bombardier's Narrative For Mission Of 22 April 1944.

TO : Commanding Officer, 100th Bombardment Group (H), Army Air Forces.

1. The C-2 and E6-B computers and A.F.C.E. were the bombing aids used.

2. A sharp turn to the left was made at the I.P.

3. Bomb bay doors were opened at 1851 at 51 43 N, 07 25 E.

4. A very short bombing run of 30 seconds was necessary. Very little evasive action was taken. The run was made manually.

5. Meager flak was the only enemy resistance encountered on the bomb run.

6. Weather was very clear on the bombing run.

7. There were no unusual tactics used by either enemy or friendly elements that hindered the bombing.

8. Visual results were not observed.

9. There was no difficulty in locating the aiming point.

10. An aiming point a little to the north of the specified aiming point was used due to the short bomb run.

11. There are no suggested tactical changes.

LESTER D. TORBETT, (Yes)
1st Lt., Air Corps,
Lead Bombardier.

Weather Mission.

April 25th 1944, our crew alone flew a flight we called a "weather mission." This was a non-combat flight and gave us no mission credit.

We were called at 1:30 a.m. and briefed to takeoff at 4:30. However the red alert sounded over the field loud speakers, which meant enemy aircraft overhead. Our takeoff was delayed waiting for the "all clear" which never came.

So regardless, we took off at 5:30 a.m. and climbed to 20,000 feet. By this time we were over London and circling in a wide area. Below us we could see the bombers starting to rise out of the murky air far below us. They were beginning to assemble their formations. This also was a sight that would never be duplicated in the years ahead.

A very spectacular sight to see hundreds of bombers forming in the early dawn. I do not recall where they were going that day, we were not going so I doubt if we knew.

The city of London was spread out below us. It was difficult to distinguish any certain area of the city, because in the early morning light, the ground 20,000 feet below us looked murky.

As I remember, the navigator was to take upper wind readings.

I had no special contacts to make, other than the normal transmissions which we held at a minimum because of all the necessary transmissions of the bombers assembling their formations.

As the bombers completed their formations and left the English coast for their targets, our task was finished. Our flight back to our base was uneventful. I remember I navigated the flight back just for practice, using our fairly new "Gee Box," an early form of radar. Our navigator had instructed me in the use of this instrument.

We landed at 9:30 a.m. This had been a four hour weather flight. We had been awake since 1:30 a.m. We received no mission credit for our efforts on this flight. Just another day of fun.

However, my next mission would be my 25th. I had no idea at this time what it would be like.

April 26th 1944, My 25th Mission.
April 26th, we were briefed for Brunswick, Germany. This would have been my final 25th mission had we not had the extended tour. This would have been the 25th that the officer so long ago had told me I probably would never reach.

On this flight the flak over the target was heavy, we had good fighter escort. Our takeoff that day was at 5 a.m. Our landing was at 12:30 p.m. another 7 1/2 hour flight.

We probably had been up since 2 a.m.

With this 25th mission completed, I had three left to finish my tour. That afternoon, I went to the radio school and talked to Captain Lash, the captain of the radio school. I wanted to be assigned as a radio instructor at the base radio school after completing my tour.

The procedure after a man completed his tour was to be assigned duties "befitting" his rank. These assignments could vary, until release papers were extended for the return to the United States. I wanted no part of an indefinite assignment. I was well acquainted with the schools operations and wanted this as a permanent assignment until my release came through.

This I presented to the captain as we sat in his office talking. This conversation was not in a military manner one sees in the movies of a T/Sgt. talking to a Captain. We were very informal.

After listening to my proposal he said, *"yes, I do need another instructor and certainly can use your experience. However the hours will be rough, you will have to report at 9 a.m. and not be through until 4 p.m."*

He well knew this was a plush job and after my long rough days of flying combat, he knew I had earned it. He added, *"finish your tour and take two weeks leave and report here as instructor."*

With this new assignment pending, I was well situated, now to finish the three missions ahead. Who knew what they would bring.

My 26th and 27th mission are described here.

The next mission was April 27th 1944. A target near Cherbourge, France. Bomb load, sixteen 300 pound demolition bombs. Now as I look back, I believe they where attempting to break up large gun emplacement before the impeding invasion. Our bombing altitude was 18,000 feet, which was extremely low for our safety. Flak was more accurate and deadly if we flew under 20,000 feet.

As we flew over this target, flak was very intense. We were hit, but not seriously and flew back to base without much trouble.

After landing from this mission to Cherbourge on April 27th, we went back to the briefing and were briefed for an airfield near Paris, France. At this time it was 3:30 p.m. The ground crews had refueled and reloaded the planes and we were scheduled to takeoff at once.

Flying over this target area we found it was overcast, making it necessary for us to bomb a secondary target. Bombs could not be dropped in France if visibility was bad over a target.

On this secondary target, light flak, nothing that caused us a problem. Missions like this one we called "milk runs." Our landing back at the base was at 9:30 p.m.

Two missions this one day, about 10 1/2 hours flying time this day. I now had one mission to fly to complete my tour.

The Day I Finished My Tour With 28 Missions.

May 1st 1944 – the day I had done the impossible, I finished the tour with 28 missions! On this, my final flight, we were briefed for an airfield near Metz, France.

Our escort was the best I had ever seen. We had P-38s, P-47s and P-51s. Complete coverage both to and from the target and all the way across the channel. In spite of all this protective coverage, four German fighters made a blazing attack, coming out of the sun and down through the tight escort we had, undetected. No damage that I heard of was done to the planes near us.

We crossed the channel safely and were making our approach to our landing. The pilot asked the engineer and I if we would care to make a low pass over the field to celebrate our completion of our tours. The flight engineer T/Sgt. Holladay and I had finished our tours today.

We both said *"land as safely as possible, no showing off."* No need to tempt fate anymore than was necessary.

I have regretted slightly in the past years that we didn't put on a show of exuberance.

As we landed safely, a fast thought entered my mind. Why did I make it through the tour and so many had not? It was a good experience to feel it was over, no need to wonder why. One great relief to me now was I could tell my parents I had completed my tour and would soon be home. I knew they had been worrying, perhaps more than I, that I would be shot down.

I now remember the words of the officer who said he doubted if any of us would complete even 25. I had completed 28 combat missions. No credit to myself, I had a good crew and lots of luck.

It had been a long way from Moses Lake, Washington. I like to call it "The Fortunes of War." Unexplainable.

T/Sgt. Earl Benham

*This photo was taken after I completed my
combat tour of 28 missions.*

*Awarded the Distinguished Flying Cross
and the Air Medal.*

"The Fortunes of War are not Understandable"

"Lucky Bastard Club"

*This certificate was presented to me on completion of
my combat tour.*

This certificate is one of a kind.

My Two Week Leave.
I was now ready to apply for my two week leave. A few days before my papers were cleared, the colonel called me to his office and asked me what I intended to do now that I had finished my tour. He said *"the war is not over and we need experienced crews."* He also said *"you will not be able to tolerate the "C.S." that you will find in the 2nd Air Force back in the States."*

I did not take his offer to fly another tour of combat. I had no intention of doing that. I thought I had pushed my luck about as far as I could expect.

After receiving my two week leave papers, I went to the beautiful city of Bournmouth, England. Located on the channel. I don't remember how long I stayed at Bournmouth. I did not seem to enjoy it much. I felt bored and could not relax, things seemed dull to me. The bombers I could see going overhead, telling me the war was not over.

I looked up at the bombers as they flew over and knew how cold it was up there. I had no desire to be up there, and yet I felt left out of the action. Glad to be safe on the ground. It was a strange mixed feeling and one I knew I must overcome.

I went to London. London always was an attraction to me. I enjoyed the balance of my two weeks there.

Crew #13 Disbanded.

When my two week leave was ended, I returned to the base. I heard that my crew members had flown a mission to Berlin while I was away. This mission proved to be a tragic one.

This was our pilots last mission, also Walts last mission of their tours. They were hit by a direct burst of flak over Berlin, this burst killed the navigator, Lt. Harold Becker, who had been with us since Moses Lake. The bombardier, Lt. Torbett also was seriously wounded. Lt. Torbett had been with us since Moses Lake.

With their oxygen gone after the flak burst., which had hit the front of the B-17, knocking out the inboard engines. This caused a considerable amount of damage, plus destroying their oxygen supply. They had to descend rapidly.

As they were descending, Walt in his tail position thought they were going to crash. He almost bailed out, but fortunately did not. This was his last mission of his tour. He would have finished with me had he not have been bumped off the crew on our lead mission to Hamm, Germany, that I have previously mentioned.

Now that they were out of formation and had to return to England alone without a navigator and the radio equipment not working and two engines gone.

A P-47 found them over the North Sea and helped guide them across the water. They eventually landed safely at our base.

Our Crew #13 was disbanded at this time. The remaining crew members had a few missions of their tours to complete. These were the veteran original crew members, Bob Goodman, "Butch" Butchino, and Jack Ogg. Torbett was grounded because of his wounds.

Our flying days as a crew were over. We had experienced a lifetime of excitement and events, since we had organized our crew at Moses Lake, Washington. We ended with one man killed and two grounded with wounds. These two eventually recovered and returned to the States.

A Story of a Mans Skill and Dedication to His Crew.
This page is an additional explanation of the last flight of Crew #13 as told on the previous page.

This report concerns the skilled and courageous action of Crew #13s flight engineer, S/Sgt. "Butch" Butchino. He and his wife Mae, live in Portland, Oregon and are long standing members of the 100th.

The story of the last combat flight of the Crew #13 of Captain Van Steenis, the mission when they were hit by flak on May 7th 1944 over Berlin. This flak killed the navigator Lt. Harold C. Becker and seriously wounded the bombardier Captain Lester D. Torbett. They came back to their base, escorted by a lone P-47 across the North Sea. They had flown all the way from Berlin with only two engines, a super job of flying by the two pilots, Captain Van Steenis and Lt. Jack Ogg.

This story has been partially written and there are some who may well remember it. However, the "rest of the story" should be told.

I had been the radio operator with this crew on my complete tour. However, I had completed my tour on May 1st with our flight engineer, Archie K. Holladay. Therefore I was not on this mission.

Being a member of this crew, I feel this story should be told. I do not know all of the detailed technical actions of the flight engineer, but will try to describe what I do know about the skill and courage displayed in this event.

S/Sgt. Butchino was asked to be the flight engineer that day by pilot Captain Van Steenis. Sgt Butchino had been with this Crew #13 since our start at Moses Lake, Washington in early 1943.

The skill and courageous service by Flight Engineer S/Sgt. "Butch" Butchino during this extreme pressure of combat, was very instrumental in saving this crew and the B-17 that day, as they made their way safely back to home base, against almost impossible odds.

After their B-17 had been hit and suffered considerable damage. Captain Van Steenis asked Sgt. Butchino to check the condition of the damage to the navigator and bombardiers compartment.

After checking that compartment, Butchino saw the navigator had been instantly killed by the blast of flak that had hit their B-17. S/Sgt Butchino then assisted the severely wounded bombardier into the radio room and applied compresses and sulfa drugs. He then instructed the two other crew men in the room to continue this procedure. This action reportedly saved the life of Captain Torbett.

Sgt Butchino surveyed the damage to the airplane and saw both inboard engines were gone. With the skill of a veteran flight engineer, which he was, he used various techniques to keep the other two engines operating. He transferred fuel from the damaged engines to the two remaining engines, this was one of the operations, as well as observing from time to time, from his upper gun turret, for possible enemy fighter attacks.

His efforts aided the pilots to keep the airplane flying across the North Sea to a safe landing at their home base at the 100th Bomb Group at Thorpe Abbotts, England.

Even after this heroic action, "Butch" Butchino continued flying combat missions until he had completed his tour. "Butch Butchino" in his modesty, never told this story. When asked to tell the entire story he says *"I only done what I was trained to do."*

This true story has certainly been lost in the records of all the many incidents of heroism of the war. This story of service that should be noticed more than it has been over the years.

Alone.

A brief description of the flight when Crew #13 were hit by flak and were coming home alone. A P-47 fighter found them alone and damaged and escorted them across the dangerous North Sea.

After their damage by flak over Berlin, they were coming back alone, carrying their dead navigator and most of their radio equipment not operating.

The name of this brave P-47 pilot who risked his own life to give them aid, is unknown to the crew to this day. His effort and dedication, is and example of the cooperation that existed between the fighter pilots and the bomber crews.

With the P-47 escorting Crew #13, they were"alone no more."

The Last Time I Saw Van.

Later our pilot Van was selected to fly non-combat for a
General. The General had completed his tour of missions

Van asked the engineer and I go with him, I gladly
would have. However this General had his engineer and
radio man who stayed with him.

I made one flight in England after completing my tour.
I was the radio operator on the plane we used to take
Van to his new assignment.

As we shook hands and said *"hope to see you again."*
I thought how little to say to a man who had taken us
through so many rough flights. What could one say?
It seemed it was impossible to say much more.
Perhaps by this time we had pushed emotions into
the background of our minds. I do not remember the
field we left him at. I knew I would remember him as a
great pilot for our crew.

Captain Loren Van Steenis

"Pilot Van" A man of cool nerve and logic.
This was a necessary attribute for a pilot flying in the
vicious tactics of aerial combat.

Van had the natural ability that helped bring our crew through
our training and through our combat tour.

I flew all of my combat flights, except one with Van at
the controls. Van was with us from our start at
Moses Lake, Washington.

Pictured here sitting on our original B-17F HARD LUCK!

My Duties as a Radio Instructor.

War was not glamorous, even though many stories try to make it appear as such, heroes to us were a dime a dozen. The acts of comradeship, the concern of each crew member for his other crew members seemed to be the most admirable attribute. What a crew members life was like, nothing before or since, has ever been quite comparable.

The days went on at Thorpe Abbotts. Much different for me now, I continued to live at the same barracks, no longer called to fly combat missions. The bombers continued to go out day after day, not always all returning.

I had started my duties as radio instructor at radio school. To me this was only a time consuming duty, while awaiting my release papers that would allow me to return to the United States.

The instructing duty consisted of giving "procedure of operation for combat flying" to new crews, also practicing operation for radio operators who were still flying combat. Training that I used to take while flying. We all knew one could not get too much practice.

The attitude of the men coming to these classes was much more mature than a regular college or high school students attitude. This was the real thing and they knew it. This practice procedure could save their lives as well as the lives of entire crew. A radio operator was needed if the airplane was forced down in the channel or North Sea. It was vital to send the correct location of the downed craft.

Often in England, flying in the common bad weather, a heading to the base was necessary. The radio operator usually had that responsibility. Morse code was the only long ranged transmissions available. Many procedures too numerous to mention here.

The "smart aleck" radio operators had long ago been left behind. The men here were the best of the lot. As I talked to these men, I often wondered how many would finish their combat tours.

Some of the events we heard from the United States would make one wonder if it were worth it all.

I spent a good part of each day at the radio school and on free time, I would visit with the ground crews there and watch the bombers returning from missions.

Usually several fighter planes would make low passes over the field, all young pilots having fun. This action could never be duplicated by the most elaborate air shows. This was the real thing and I felt to a certain degree that I was part of it all, even though in a small way.

Being in the service in England was far more social than many of the war areas. I had made several trips to London, Norwich, Oxford etc. The life while not flying was almost as if there were no war. The English country was beautiful, I could almost visualize myself living here on a permanent basis.

The bombing attacks on England were diminished now, a few buzz bombs coming over. I think our bombing of their coastal installations had curtailed the forces.

The latest news was the Germans were about to introduce a new weapon. This was the larger rocket than the winged V-1 or "buzzbomb." This was called the V-2.

This was launched from a gantry and would ascend many miles into the upper stratosphere and come down at tremendous speed and hit with devastating explosive force. There was no known defense against this type of bomb because of the speed involved.

The rocket used to propel this bomb was a forerunner of the rockets developed many years later, after we were able to hire the German rocket scientists. The United States did not have this knowledge as yet.

Germany now, in almost the final stages of the war, were ahead of us in the development of rockets. They had the enlisted efforts of many of the worlds rocket scientists

Germany was about ready to introduce the new jet fighter airplane against our air force with dire results. We did not have the faster jet aircraft yet. Germany was also ahead of us on this development, I often wondered just were we stood.

Germany had attempted to conquer the world, and if they had not attacked Russia, I believed they could have done that very thing. The war Germany started with Russia gave us the time to develop and finally able to get started defending our country's interests, by using England as a landing field for our bombers.

Without our heavy bombers ability to bomb German installations, we undoubtably would have felt German atomic bombs falling in America.

People even to this day do not seem to realize how really close they were to a possible annihilation. We had nothing to defend ourselves from the German rockets and nothing to retaliate with equal force. Many of the people living in the United States were totally ignorant of the powerful organization of the German forces.

This attitude I noticed when I was employed by the Consolidated Aircraft plant in San Diego before I entered the Service. People thought they were patriotic when thy bought "War Bonds" and while in defense plants if they worked overtime (for overtime pay) and would meet the production schedule, they would perhaps get a plaque of "E" for effort. Much like Boy and Girl Scouts.

What was war all about? This seemed a question for many people and certainly to some the question, "where is Germany?"

I never could understand the necessity for our country to entice or entertain people to "Buy War Bonds." Unless it was meant to them a feeling they were sacrificing for their country. Certainly no sacrifice to the people who bought the bonds. They were well paid with good interest on their money.

What this country needed then were people who were willing to fight for their country, even if it took 100 hours a week of their time, without pay. It took real men like the ones I knew, to win the war.

The French nation was easily conquered by the German Army. However, many of the more patriotic French people fought as underground agents against German forces, at great risk to their lives and to the lives of their families

We had many flyers shot down over enemy territory who were rescued by these French patriots. These flyers would otherwise have been POWs. Patriotism certainly was more than buying war bonds or working to get a plaque of "E" for effort.

D-Day, The Invasion of Normandy.

One evening in June of 1944, I was asked to stand guard at one of the gun pits we had. I believe we had about a dozen of these .50 caliber machine gun pits. A single .50 caliber machine gun mounted in sandbagged pits, located around the field. A completely inadequate defense, however it was all we had.

I was not accustomed to standing guard, this was the second time I had done this, it was a cold damp night. We had been briefed that a German parachute attack was possible, we were not impressed. One other fellow and I were stationed at this post about 10:00 p.m.

About midnight I noticed an unusual amount of activity, many trucks in motion around the area where we were, near the flight line.Many airplanes being tested, I just figured a big mission was being scheduled.

Near dawn the airplanes began taking off. That morning I counted fifty four B-17s taking off about one minute apart. I had never seen so many in one group before. I realized this was the largest group ever to leave our field on one mission. Another sight that would never be duplicated.

After the planes had left, the jeep came out to take us back and to the mess hall for breakfast. After breakfast I talked to some people about the mission, no one knew what was going on.

I thought the security of the base was good, at least today. I then went back to the barracks and went to sleep. I had been up all night.

I was sleeping soundly at 10:00 a.m. when I was suddenly awakened by a crew member from our barracks who just returned from the early morning flight. He shook me awake shouting *"Get up, this is D-DAY!"*

The description of what they had seen of the invasion were almost unbelievable. Many men had been killed that morning as I slept, the invasion forces had "hit the beaches." Again the fortunes of war, unbelievable.

Our group along other heavy bombers, flew what they called tactical support for the ground troops invading France at this time. The tactical support was of short duration, probably three or four days. The heavy bombers went back to the strategic as before the invasion, leaving tactical bombing to the smaller bombers and other aircraft.

The war seemed to be coming to an end, but a long way to go yet. We could not know what success the invading forces would have.

The events of Thorpe Abbotts continued at normal levels. We continued to lose airplanes and flight crews. Flying bombing missions was a very hazardous endeavor.

I continued to work at the radio school. I had recently been advised by the major and the captain of the school, that I should become a communication officer. They said if I chose to do so they would help me enter that field. I also could possibly continue as instructor at this school at Thorpe Abbotts.

One problem bothered me, and that was I would be signed up for the duration of the war in England, with no leave to return to the United States as I was scheduled for.

At this time I had no idea how much longer the war would last. I did seriously consider this offer and decided not to take it. Later in life as I looked back, I believe I could have had the officers extend my leave from the 100th and waited for my return and have continued on with my proposed promotion. This I did not do, which has been one of my life's regrets.

I think William Butler Yeats who once said *"Time and the world are ever in flight."* Therefore we sometimes let the world pass us by and we are left with some regret.

Leaving the 100th Bomb Group, En route to the U.S.A.

I think on July 20th, Holladay and I were called to the operations office to sign our release papers. We were on our way to the United States. One thing I noticed, there was no band assembled to give us a rousing send off.

In fact I thought perhaps few people knew, or cared if we left or stayed at the field. I knew there were many assignments more important to be considered by those who were still actively engaged in the war.

Holladay and I were now "has beens" our days on the ETO were over, at least for the present. At this time we thought we may be returned later if the war continued for another year.

I packed my bags getting ready to leave. I wanted to take with me a few items for souvenirs. My British helmet, my oxygen mask, my Mae West life jacket, I had worn it on every one of my missions as we flew over water on every mission. My flying boots, my Colt .45 pistol. So many items I wanted to keep.

Holladay and I were now ready to leave. We perhaps said goodbye to some, I do not recall that we did.

I think at this time we were not very sentimental. We were leaving a place, we later learned, that would be dismantled. This was our last view of it as we knew it then. The base was dismantled after the war, at least most of it.

The experiences we had been through at this base were overwhelming. In later years I realized many memories of people we had met over there. I have often thought of retuning to these scenes of my youth, even though the scenes are now completely changed. Returning to the "scenes of ones youth" could be disappointing. However, the skies over England are the same ones that we flew through so often and much of the beautiful countryside must yet be the same.

Boarding the Ship.
We arrived at a processing center near Liverpool, England. The name of the place was Chorley. We left Chorley on the 21st to go to a base about eight miles from there. We returned to Chorley on July 28th and processed our gear for the trip to the United States.

The following day we were briefed about the procedure we were to use. We were going to make the trip by boat. I had hoped we would fly, there would be submarines in the Atlantic and I had no desire to encounter one of those.

Our ship was a luxury liner called "West Point." This ship in civilian days was called the "United States." The ship was fast enough to elude submarines. However, they were taking the northern route across the Atlantic and using some evasive action which would take an extra day of travel. The trip would take six days, instead of the normal five.

After our briefing we went outside, the officer in charge explained what we were authorized to bring with us. After reviewing the list, I noticed all of the items I wanted to bring were banned.

The procedure was to line up our bags for inspection and in the interval before inspection, we were given the opportunity to discard all banned items into the ever growing pile.

When the bags were inspected, if any of the banned items were still in our bag, we could have our shipping orders delayed. The officer made it quite clear when he said *"you are all grown men and know what is expected of you."* Naturally I threw all of my banned items in the pile.

However, the irony was, just before my bags were inspected it started to rain harder. The inspector said *"close them all up and we can get out of this rain."* I could have had all my items. My bags were never inspected.

July 28th, we went to Liverpool to board ship. We were boarded quite late in the day. It was my first experience in such a large ship. The size was startling. I think it was 1,000 feet long.

Holladay and I were assigned to a cabin (room). This was paneled and on an outside wall of the ship. We had a port hole to look through, I think we were only one story down from the deck. This would be a luxury room for civilian travel. The ship was not crowded, that is why we had such nice quarters.

It being late, I went to bed and decided to explore the ship the next day. We were in the harbor until quite late.

I went to sleep before they left port.

Leaving England.

I arose quite early the next morning and went out on deck. The cool air from the ocean was very invigorating. I noticed we were well out into the north Atlantic.

England was disappearing into the misty horizon. I had a brief feeling of nostalgia or perhaps more of a longing to someday return.

I thought of the many people I had known, even though briefly. I thought of the devastation of the war and that what I had seen of it would, hopefully never have to be duplicated. Yet I knew the war was not over.

I thought also of the men in our Crew #13. This morning seemed to me the ending of our start from Moses Lake. My thoughts were, would I ever see any of them again.

In my estimation, the war could not have been won without the efforts of men like these. There were many men in the Air Force of this caliber. This was one reason a man could be proud to have been a small part of it.

The Members of Crew #13.

Pilot, Captain Loren C. Van Steenis

He remained in the Air Force for some time after returning to the States. He later was employed by the Tennessee Valley Electric Company. He was living at Hartsel, Alabama. He passed away from a heart attack in 1985.

Co-Pilot, Lt. Jack Ogg

Was employed by a computer company. Later, in the real estate business. Presently retired and living in Desert Hot Springs, California.

Navigator, Lt. Harold Becker

Killed in action on May 7th 1944 on a mission to Berlin, Germany.

Bombardier, Captain Lester D. Torbett

Grounded by wounds on May 7th 1944 on a mission to Berlin. After extensive hospitalization, he was released from the Air Force. He had a Masters Degree in business and was employed with a large company. Formerly a resident of Oklahoma, he was living in Texas at the time of his death in 1963.

Flight Engineer, T/Sgt. Archie K. Holladay

Living in Manning, South Carolina. He has been self-employed for years, now semi-retired.

Assistant Flight Engineer, S/Sgt. Edward C. Butchino
Was employed as a dispatcher for the Power Electrical Company of Oregon for 30 years. Now retired and living in Portland, Oregon.

Tail Gunner, S/Sgt. Walter A. Schneider
Employed by a company in Massachusetts. He was a M/Sgt. in the Army Reserves. Now retired and living in Colrain, Massachusetts.

Armorer/Gunner, S/Sgt James Yarnell
Employed by company in Wormleysburg, Pennsylvania. He passed away July 29th 1992.

Ball Turret Gunner, S/Sgt. Robert Goodman
Employed as a college professor in Columbia, Missouri. He was a Lt. Colonel in the Army Reserves. Now retired and living in Columbia, Missouri.

Radio Operator, T/Sgt. Earl V. Benham
Owned and operated an Auto Parts business in Minnesota. Later employed at the U.S. Post Office in Phoenix, Arizona. Now retired and living in Phoenix, Arizona.

Lt. Jack Ogg

Jack trained in the U.S.A with his flight crew and flew to England in 1943. Upon arriving, the crew was separated and each member was assigned to other combat crews.

Jack arrived at the 100th Bomb Group and was assigned to "The Van Steenis Crew" as Co-Pilot. He flew with Crew #13 until we completed our tour of missions.

He then flew the remainder of his mission tour as First Pilot with green crews, giving them the benefit of his combat experience.

He completed his tour and returned to the U.S.A. where he flew as an Instructor Pilot on B-25s.

S/Sgt. Walter Schneider

Walt trained in Gunnery School as an Armorer/Gunner. After graduation he was sent to Moses Lake, Washington. There he was assigned to "The Van Steenis Crew."

Walt was qualified for any gun position on the B-17 and chose the Tail Gunner position. He flew with our crew as Tail Gunner and Formation Observer.

He flew with Crew #13 his full tour of missions and completed them on May 7th 1944 after the tragic last flight mentioned on page 128.

Walt returned to the U.S.A. and later became a M/Sgt. in the Army Reserves.

Crew #13...1943

Top Row L-R: T/Sgt. "Hap" Holladay, S/Sgt. Bob Goodman,
S/Sgt. Jim Yarnell, S/Sgt. Clothier (took Jim's Yarnell's place),
S/Sgt. Walt Schneider, S/Sgt. Edward "Butch" Butchino,
T/Sgt. Earl Benham.

Bottom Row L-R: Lt. Jack Ogg, Capt. Loren Van Steenis,
Lt. Harold Becker, Lt. Les Torbett.

Crew #13...1991
Top Row L-R: Butch Butchino, Hap Holladay,
Walt Schneider, Jack Ogg.

Bottom Row L-R: Earl Benham, Bob Goodman.

In Conclusion.

When one reviews the description or events of the story of these missions, we must be reminded of the terrible destructive forces involved. We were faced with an enemy who started the war with destructive force. We retaliated with an even greater destructive force, to the conclusion of the war.

The men flying combat missions were faced with many different situations. Some very tragic experiences for many of these men. These experiences were different than they had ever faced. Yet these young men did face them.

Now, time has diminished many of these feelings and emotions of those difficult days. As new generations develop, memories of these missions will further dim into the background of life and will in many instances be forgotten, or even unknown.

A few pages of literature such as this will remain for verification. For many, to view these events, if only in retrospect and wonder...to always wonder.

Full Record of Mission Tour.

November 1943 through May 1944.
This is a brief description of each flight taken from
my diary written at the time.

Nov 1943 Our first mission, scrubbed just before takeoff.

Nov 5, 1943 Briefed for Gelsenkirchen, Germany. We flew as spares. Bomb load: eight 500 lb. demos. Engine problem on takeoff. Oxygen leak at 20,000 ft. We returned to base. No mission credit.

Nov 7, 1943 Briefed for Duren, Germany. Bomb load: demos & incendiaries. Incident: nine bombs failed to release from bomb racks. S/Sgt. Butchino & Sgt. Yarnell released them into the channel on our way back.

Nov 16, 1943 Briefed for Rjukan, Norway. Target was a hydro-electric plant which was storing heavy water used in the production of the atom bomb. Target destroyed. I sent the strike report to England from the target area.

Nov 19, 1943 Briefed for Gelsenkirchen, Germany. Bomb load: demos. We took off in cloudy weather. Target overcast. Mission led by Pathfinder.

Nov 26, 1943 Briefed for an airfield near Paris, France. Bomb load: twelve 500 lb. demos. Target overcast, could not drop bombs on France if target was not visible. Flak over target heavy. Some German fighters. We landed with full bomb load.

Nov 29, 1943 Briefed for Bremen, Germany. Several enemy fighters. We were attacked by FW-190s. We had P-47 escort.

Nov 30, 1943 Briefed for Solingen, Germany. Our pilot passed out at 18,000 ft. from oxygen failure. We returned to base after we salvoed the bombs in channel.

Dec 5, 1943 Briefed for Bordeaux, France. Pathfinder lead. Target overcast. No bomb release. We brought bombs back to our base.

Dec 10, 1943 We flew as spares. No place to fill in. We dropped bombs in channel. No mission credit.

Dec 13, 1943 Briefed for Kiel, Germany. We flew as spares. No place to fill in. We returned to base. Landed with bombs. No mission credit.

Dec 14, 1943 Briefed for Berlin, Germany. Mission scrubbed just before takeoff. We were again briefed for Kiel, Germany, this was also canceled before takeoff.

Dec 16, 1943 Briefed for Bremen, Germany. Bomb load: eight 500 lb. demos and twenty incendiary bombs. We flew as spares. We had a runaway supercharger at takeoff. We landed after two attempts in bad weather, fog and rain. We changed to a different airplane and took off. No place to fill in the formation. We returned to base. Landed in fog and rain with full bomb load. No mission credit.

Dec 22, 1943 Briefed for Munster, Germany. Full load if incendiaries. Pathfinder lead. We took off in rain. Complete overcast over target. Light flak. P-47 & P-38 escort.

Dec 24, 1943 Target near Abbeville and Dieppi, France. Bomb load: 300 lb. demos. Altitude over target: 12,000 ft. Our base was fogged in on our return. We had a difficult time landing.

Dec 29, 1943   Briefed for Ludwigshafen, Germany. Bomb load: incendiaries. We flew as spares. Took off at 8:30 a.m. No place to fill in the formation. We returned to base. Landed with full bomb load. No mission credit. (4 hours)

Jan 4, 1944   Briefed for Kiel, Germany. Bomb load: ten 500 lb. demos. Pathfinder lead. Target overcast. Altitude 29,000 ft. over target. Flak very heavy and accurate.

Jan 5, 1944   Target: Elbepild, Germany. Target was a ball bearing plant. We diverted by bad weather, to the secondary target of Nuess, Germany. This was a nut & bolt factory of great importance. We bombed from 26,000 ft. Temperature -52 degrees below zero. Flak very heavy. Our P-47 escort good. (5:50 hours)

Jan 7, 1944   Target Ludwigshafen, Germany. This was a chemical plant, a power dam and a rubber plant. Pathfinder lead. Bomb load: ten 500 lb. demos. Flak thick over target. P-47 & Spitfire escort. Target destroyed, bombing altitude 26,000 ft. One bomb failed to release over target. Sgts. Butchino and Yarnell released it over the channel. Our base was closed by fog, I helped bring us over the field by radio. (7:30 hours)

Jan 15, 1944   Target Halberstadt, Germany. Mission canceled just before takeoff.

Jan 20, 1944   Target installations on French coast. Canceled just before takeoff.

Jan 21, 1944   Briefed for installations on French coast. Bombed from 20,000 ft. Six plane formation. Each six planes made separate runs. Flak very heavy. Our plane hit several times. (7 hours)

Jan 24, 1944   Target Frankfurt, Germany. We took off at 7 a.m. Heavy contrails at 15,000 ft. made grouping the formations difficult. We were 150 miles over enemy territory when we were recalled to base We came out across Holland, would not bomb Holland blind, we dropped the bombs in the channel. Very bad weather at our base prevented us landing with the bombs in the airplanes. (5:50 hours)

Jan 26, 1944   Briefed for Frankfurt, Germany. Mission scrubbed before takeoff. Another briefing for French coast also scrubbed later.

Jan 21, 1944   Part of crew flew to a field near Cambridge. We took another pilot there on business.

Jan 31, 1944   Briefed for Frankfurt, Germany. Scrubbed 30 minutes before takeoff.

Feb 4, 1944   Briefed for Frankfurt, Germany. Bomb load: ten 500 lb. demos. Pathfinder lead. Bombed from 25,000 ft. Ground speed 300 mph over target. Flak very thick, some enemy fighter attacks. We had a rough time landing at our base because of weather and cross winds. This was the one, and only time I flew a mission without Van at the controls. Van was off with a bad cold. He missed this mission and this nearly cost him his life. (7:30 hours)

Feb 8, 1944   We flew a short practice formation flight. (4 hours)

Feb 9, 1944   Target Halberstadt, Germany. We took off at 7 a.m. and were recalled at 8:15 because of bad weather. We landed at 10 a.m. with full bomb load. No mission credit.

Feb 11, 1944   We flew another short formation flight. (4 hours)

Feb 8, 1944	We flew a short practice formation flight. (4 hours)
Feb 9, 1944	Target Halberstadt, Germany. We took off at 7 a.m. and were recalled at 8:15 because of bad weather. We landed at 10 a.m. with full bomb load. No mission credit.
Feb 11, 1944	We flew another short formation flight. (4 hours)
Feb 12, 1944	We flew a practice formation flight. (4 hours)
Feb 13, 1944	We bombed installations on the French coast. Flak very accurate, bursting close to our plane. Bombing altitude 12,000 ft. Good fighter escort. (3:30 hours)
Feb 15, 1944	Flew a practice formation flight. (4 hours)
Feb 21, 1944	Target Brunswick, Germany. Pathfinder lead. Bombed airfield and railroad marshalling yards. Light flak, very good escort. Bombing altitude 22,000 ft. (7 hours)
Feb 22, 1944	Briefed for Schwienfurt, Germany. Bomb load: ten 500 lb. demos. We took off in snow flurries. Gained altitude to 22,000 ft. Heavy contrails made grouping difficult. Visibility zero at times. We were recalled because of bad weather. Landed at base with full bomb load. No mission credit.
Feb 23, 1944	Briefed for Schwienfurt, Germany. Mission scrubbed after being postponed 1 hour.
Feb 24, 1944	Target Posen, Poland. Bomb load: ten 500 lb. demos. We were attacked by German fighter planes over Denmark. The weather prevented us from reaching Posen. We were near, we changed course and bombed Rostock, Germany. There was heavy flak over Rostock. We had

more attacks by German fighter planes on the way out. Our airplane was hit. Our waist gunner S/Sgt. Yarnell was wounded in the shoulder and the right hand. We landed okay at our base. This had been a rough 11 hour flight. S/Sgt. Yarnell was grounded because of his wounds. (11 hours)

Feb 25, 1944   Briefed for Regensburg, Germany. Bomb load: ten 500 lb. demos. Target hit in clear visibility. Good fighter escort, heavy flak over target. We were hit several times. We came back to base with three engines. Our base was badly closed with fog for a landing. (9:30 hours)

Feb 26, 1944   Briefed for Friedrichshafen, Germany. Bomb load: forty two 100 lb. incendiaries. Mission canceled just before takeoff.

After this time our crew went on a nine day leave.

Mar 14, 1944   We flew a practice flight.

Mar 15, 1944   We flew a practice flight.

Mar 16, 1944   Our crew test flew a new airplane. We called the plane "HARD LUCK 2". We were now a "Group Lead Crew."

Mar 17, 1944   Target Oberpfaffenhofen, Germany, with Munich as secondary target. These missions were canceled at takeoff time. We returned to the briefing room and were briefed for Frankfurt, Germany. This was also canceled just before takeoff because of fog.

Mar 18, 1944   Briefed for an airfield and installations five miles north of Augsburg, Germany. Bomb load: ten 500 lb. demos. Our plane hit by flak as we crossed the French coast on the way in. Torbett, our bombardier was hit and was not able to operate his bombsight. We were flying group lead. We left the formation and returned to base. (4:30 hours)

Mar 25, 1944 We flew a practice formation flight.

Mar 26, 1944 Target Leipzig, Germany. A factory making JU-88s. We were scheduled to lead group. Mission canceled at takeoff time. We had been up since 2 a.m. We flew a practice 4 hour flight that afternoon.

Mar 27, 1944 Briefed for an airfield 15 miles from Bordeaux, France We flew lead. Bomb load: ten 500 lb. demos. Flak very heavy over target. Bombing altitude 23,000 ft. We hit the target with good concentration. The 8th Air Force bombed several targets in that area that day. We saw smoke from several areas. (9 hours)

Apr 7, 1944 Briefed for Quackenbruck, Germany. Mission canceled just before takeoff.

Apr 8, 1944 Briefed for Quackenbruck again. Target an airfield. Bomb load: thirty eight 100 lb. bombs. Bombing altitude 20,000 ft. Good fighter escort.

Apr 9, 1944 Briefed for an aircraft factory at Posen, Poland. Bomb load: incendiaries. We took off in bad weather, formations were split up over the North Sea in heavy clouds. The group could not reform. We returned to England alone and could not land at our base because of bad weather. We landed at a B-24 base. Returned later to our base as weather cleared that day. No mission credit.

Apr 11, 1944 Briefed for Posen Poland again. Bomb load: five 1000 lb. demos. Took off at 7 a.m. We flew across the North Sea in very bad weather, formations were badly formed as we crossed the coast of Denmark. We met strong formations of German fighter planes. Many B-17s were lost. The target at Posen was overcast. We changed course and again bombed the marshalling yards at Rostock, Germany.

Flak very heavy over Rostock. We met German fighter planes on our way out. We landed at our base at 5 p.m. The field was closed in with clouds. This was a long, rough mission of 10 hours. A mission similar to Feb 24th when Jim was injured.

Apr 18, 1944 Our crew flew a practice mission.

Apr 20, 1944 Briefed for installations on French coast. Bomb load: twelve 500 lb. demos and two 1,000 lb. demos under wings. We took off at 4 p.m. The two 1,000 lb. bombs were attached to the underside of the wings, one on each side. The first and only time we carried them that way. Flak over target was very heavy and accurate. We landed at our base at 8:35 p.m.

Apr 22, 1944 Briefed for Hamm, Germany. Target, the railroad marshalling yards. Bomb load: ten 500 lb. demos. Bombing altitude 23,000 ft. Flak very heavy over target. We had good fighter escort. Our crew led the group and most of the 8th Air Force. Our Group C.O. Colonel Kelly flew with us as an observer. Our Squadron C.O. Major Elton flew with us as co-pilot. Our regular co-pilot flew as tail gunner. We took off at 3 p.m. Landing at 9:30 p.m.

Apr 24, 1944 We flew a 4 hour practice mission.

Apr 25, 1944 Our crew flew a weather mission for the group. A non-combat flight. We were called up at 1:45 a.m. Briefed to take off at 4:30 a.m. An air raid alert delayed our takeoff until 5:30 a.m. We took off and climbed to 20,000 ft. over London. After the bombers had left England, we returned to base at 9:30 a.m.

Apr 26, 1944   Briefed for Brunswick, Germany. Bomb load: 42 incendiaries. Pathfinder lead. We took off at 5:10 a.m. Flak very heavy over target. We had good escort. Landed back at base at 12:20 p.m.

Apr 27, 1944   Target near Cherbourg, France. Bomb load: sixteen 300 lb. armor piercing bombs. Altitude over target 18,000 ft. Flak very heavy. We returned to base and were briefed for a second mission that day. Target was an airfield near Paris, France. Bomb load twelve 500 lb. demos. We took off at 3:30 p.m. Heavy flak over target. we bombed the secondary target as primary was overcast. Landed at base at 9:30 p.m The two missions this one day totaled 10:30 hours flying time.

May 1, 1944   Briefed for Metz, France. Rail;road marshalling yard. Bomb load: six 1,000 lb. demos. Took off at 3:30 p.m. Fighter escort very good. We had full coverage with P-38s, P-51s and P-47s. Some light flak over target. Four enemy fighters made a blazing attack at our group. We landed okay at our base. This was my 28th and last mission.

On May 1st 1944, I had completed my officially required tour of 28 combat flight missions.

Luck had been with me, as well a super flight crew and a super ground crew of mechanics.

I had reason to wonder why I had completed my tour and so many had not. This would be a wonder I could not explain....I was not asked to explain

– Earl Benham

*My A-2 leather jacket that I wore on all of my
combat missions with the hand painted
art of HARD LUCK!*

After 60 years, though somewhat worn, it still looks good.

A Trip Back to Thorpe Abbotts
57 Years Later...

Having written the book "With Crew #13" as an experience of flying with this one crew. Starting from our first as a new crew in training in the United States, and followed by a tour of combat flying with the 100th Bomb Group at Thorpe Abbotts, England.

In September 2001 after 57 years, I returned to Thorpe Abbotts, the WWII home of the 100th Bomb Group. This trip was one that only a former combat air crew veteran could fully appreciate. I was accompanied on this trip by Scott Smith who is well versed in the history of the 100th Bomb Group. Therefore, he also was highly interested in taking this trip even though he of the next generation.

To begin this story of my trip back, I would like to start where I left off in the in the first book. I ended by telling of my first morning on the ship bringing me home to the United States from England. I mentioned that first early morning on the ship and seeing the coast of England fading away in the distance. It was late July 1944 and I was on my way home after completing my tour of missions in England. I wondered would I ever return was a thought in my mind at that time.

Realizing today the time of 57 years has slipped away rapidly, events occurred too numerous to completely write about, some of the highlights can be mentioned here.

I well remember the drastic change of returning to civilian life after the three years of my military career. My term of military service was short compared to many others. In fact my brother spent four years in military service as a draftee, and three full years in the South Pacific area without a furlough back to the United States during that entire time.

I was fortunate spending only one year over seas away from home, spending that year in England where living conditions were great and far better than most military locations.

Upon my return to the United States I had a thirty day leave to reassignment. This gave me the opportunity to be married, and in so doing I took the chance my military service would be secure enough to warrant marriage, with its future.

The fact now, as I recall, I then perhaps was highly optimistic, that is now my viewpoint of that decision.

I next was sent to Miami Beach, Florida, staying at the then luxurious Traymore Hotel for three weeks of testing and orientation for further assignment.

This resulted in finally my selection to be a radio instructor at military radio schools. I continued at this duty until my military discharge. the location of these schools were at Sioux Falls, South Dakota and Truax field at Madison, Wisconsin.

One ironic part I will recall here. This occasion occurred one week before my point credit would allow my military discharge. To now explain this irony.

I was informed the Air Force wanted twenty qualified radio operators to fly as radio operators in the C-54, a huge four engine cargo plane. The ironic part, was that it should be offered to me a week before my military discharge was to be effective. This assignment on C-54s I had wanted for quite some time.

With the thought of possibly signing up for this request I went to the meeting. There at the meeting I was told this offer required a four year of duty. I thought rapidly and asked for a two day extension that I may deliberate the possibility of signing for another four year term of duty.

This request was denied and the order was *"to be ready to move out the very next morning at 6 a.m."* They asked for twenty volunteers and two spares in the event some did not appear that next morning.

I thought as I had always, in my Air Force career, "let fate be the judge." Therefore, I would do so in this situation as well. The program called for two spares should someone fail to be on call. I volunteered to be listed as a spare and would go provided that was the selection and the will of fate.

That early morning in freezing cold I was ready to go, and on time. The entire twenty men arrived, therefore no spares were needed. I returned to my barracks, unable in my mind to determine seriously if I was happy or sad at the turn of events. I had rather hoped to be selected.

My military discharge came as planned and I was out of the service one week later, fate had been the deciding factor. To this day, 57 years later, I wonder as I look at a C-54 with some thought of what might have been.

Returning to civilian life I often thought of the days I had spent at the 100th Bomb Group. Days that were etched in memory, memories of the events that are unexplainable. Memories of comrades that are no longer here, however, are thought of at times.

I recalled unnamed faces of men I vaguely knew, now with regrets. Because we did not keep records of very many. Names were only known as maybe a nickname or Joe or Jack etc.

Our crew of ten men were special in our memory. Fortunately, I had completed my tour with this one crew and never had to fly with or be assigned to another crew.

Today as I write this addition to this book, there are only four men remaining of the original crew of ten men. This does offer some "thought and reflection" that only men of a loyal combat flight crew can understand fully, in this same light concerning many associations, and of the 100th Bomb Group.

With this thought in mind I considered, over the many years, of returning to the old base of the 100th Bomb Group, and to the scenes of my youth. However, knowing full well it no longer would be the same airfield. I knew vast changes have been made, and most of the airfield has returned to agriculture as it was prior to the war. The very same fields of farmland so much needed by Britain, now are the same farmland that had been given to the site of the airfield, and of the massive amounts of concrete which had to be removed from the airfield to restore the land back to agricultural use.

Therefore, now realizing these many changes may defeat the pleasant thought of returning there. This was a thought with which I seemed to be concerned.

Why return to destroy the image in my mind of this huge working bomber base as I knew it in the days I had seen it last, 57 years ago?

Our crew mate, Robert Goodman, had made a brief visit to the base in 1969 and was very disappointed at the decrepit condition of the field he had once known.

He said instead of B-17s sitting on the hardstands, they now were piled high with refuse. Therefore, in his evaluation, it was disheartening, and a sight he did not care to witness. The "scenes of his youth" as he recalled, were disappointing to him then.

England is a rather small country, and to have sacrificed so many acres of their farmland to allow these many bomber bases to have been constructed tells of their dedication, and of the necessity to fight a huge war.

People who lived in other countries then, even today, seem not to fully realize what had been required of the British people.

Thinking of these various aspects of returning to the old bomber base, I had heard later from reliable sources, the Control Tower which was still standing, was being salvaged and restored by a group of dedicated volunteers, and the intent was to restore is as a museum for the remembrance of the 100th Bomb Group.

Other buildings in the surrounding area were also being salvaged. This was encouraging news that seemed to be happening, but we really didn't know much about it.

Over the past years I talked to various people who had visited the now partially developed museum. I later talked to two of the men in our crew, Butch Butchino and Walter Schneider who had visited the museum several years ago. Our former co-pilot Jack Ogg mentioned he had visited the area twice in later years and our flight engineer Archie Holladay also had visited a few years ago.

They all seemed quite impressed with the reconstructed Control Tower. When talking with them, they tried to explain to me how the base appeared to them.

I finally knew I would have to see it for myself, and to again feel the sense of nostalgia as I often had when thinking of the days when it was an active bomber base.

I have often thought being a member of a flight crew was an experience which nothing before or since has been quite comparable.

Right or wrong, we had a job to do that seemed at the time, to be all encompassing.

Much respect for the men of our crew. A respect that derived its object from seeing these men in real danger, and knowing they were men who had no intention of evading what they considered their shared duty to their country, and to their fellow crew mates. To belong to a flight crew was a voluntary assignment and of that I am sure we all were proud.

With this thought in mind it seemed fitting to again return to the area which had occupied this short period of time in my life, and seemed to have left so many memories.

Therefore, to again walk in the same area, regardless of the apparent changes. This I considered could be inspiring and certainly nostalgic in my reflections of the past.

Knowing we do not, or should not, be too engrossed with the past, we must however, have certain recollections of the past which we could reestablish in our thoughts.

Thereby, bringing some thoughts back, and possibly a renewed concept. Thus returning to the old bomber base may give one that effect. To see it again as it is now, actually in the present. The old "war days" then possibly could be seen in a different light, yet retaining the certain degree of nostalgia and remembrance of what used to be.

This seemed a logical reason to again consider returning. However, realizing never again the actual situation I once knew could ever possibly be duplicated. We also would feel fortunate that never would bombers fly at war again from this field as they once did.

With some of this in mind, I decided to return to Thorpe Abbotts to revisit my old 100th Bomb Group base. Now called the 100th Bomb Group Memorial Museum. This return was to be 57 years after I had left in late July 1944.

Leaving for England Again.
Now today I was flying in a Boeing 777 rather than in a Boeing B-17. This now was a non-stop 10-hour flight from Phoenix, Arizona. The flight time was comparable to a mission we flew to Posen, Poland in 1944 in the B-17. The great difference was the fact we now flew in solid comfort in the 777.

To make a comparison to the B-17, using oxygen masks most all the way, no food, no flight attendants, heavy flak over targets, fighter attacks along some of the way, temperatures in the minus degrees, perhaps 45 below zero at altitude, the flight over the North sea was always treacherous.

This nostalgic remembrance was with me on this modern day flight. As I looked down at the southern coast of Greenland, I recalled that we had landed there on our flight to England in 1943, 58 years ago, with our faithful B-17. I understood and could realize now on this trip, of 57 years later, was promising to be one of many memories.

Landing in London.

As we approached the landing area in London, I looked down at the beautiful English countryside which looked familiar, the same as I had frequently looked down upon it from the B-17 those many years ago. Now after 57 years I was back again.

Prior to my leaving for England I was told by several people, quote: *"I bet you will be happy to meet all your friends when you arrive."* The part they did not understand was the fact I only had officially met three people who would be there. They were Ron and Carol Batley, Ron is the Chairman of the 100th Bomb Group Memorial Museum Organization. I had previously met them when they had made a trip to the U.S.A. I had also met Ron Leigh, an accomplished painter on a trip he had made there as well. The people I had vaguely known so long ago were not on my mind to be met here.

In the action of combat flying, the people we knew as friends were few and far between, as most did not stay long enough to become very well acquainted. As I have previously mentioned, I vaguely knew several men we flew with.

Now quite recently, possibly only the past six or seven years, I had met several people from England by way of email, and had letters and telephone calls from others associated with the museum. They said *"they would have the Red Carpet out for us."*

Now to establish some personal notes about people who were very courteous and cooperative, and sincerely generous, who gave me a great welcome. The first I will mention is Stephan Page and his son John, who volunteered to meet us at the airport and gave us a ride to Diss, where I had reserved a B&B for two days.

This was the first leg of the trip after arriving in England. I will list Stephan here because he was the first of the many, many acts of generosity of many people involved to make my stay a great experience.

That in its self is a complete story, and perhaps I shall not tell of each individual offer of their cooperation in this book. They are the volunteers who have made it all possible, a story in itself. Their acts of generosity of their time and efforts to show me all around the area. Without their efforts, my trip back after 57 years would not have been a success. I can again tell them all "Thank You" at this writing, I will list all their names at the conclusion of the book.

Now looking at the event of actually being back again at the 100th Bomb Group was an exciting time and one I realized I had looked forward to for so many years.

Back to Thorpe Abbotts.

Stephan Page arrived at the Bed and Breakfast that first morning and gave us a ride to the base. There I was met first by Carol Batley who took me to the door of the Varian Center where I met Gordon Dickie and Ken Everett. The welcome was light and cordial and I had the inspiration that I now could certainly feel "as if I really had returned."

I entered the building and met several volunteers. I was amazed at the beautiful displays in the building, the wall decorations and paintings of B-17s I had read about, some I knew personally. The neat and clean appearance of it all plus the beautiful mural painted by a professional lady artist was all outstanding to me.

The painting covers the entire end wall of the interior of the Varian Center. This was my first impression to the 100th Bomb Group Memorial Museum, and I am sure to many other visitors. Carol Batley spoke up saying, *"this evening you are coming to my home for dinner."*

The Bridge in Norwich.

All of this so far is just a small indication of the cordial treatment we received. This was day one. A bit later that day, now having met Mike Plummer, a volunteer, he said *"tomorrow morning I am picking you both up and we are giving you a tour of Norwich,"* a city in which he lives. Plus, he added *"you will be having dinner at our home."*

What could be a better way for me to again visit Norwich, than a tour extended to me by a person who is acquainted with the city and the cordial invitation to their home where we met Mrs. Plummer. With this tour of Norwich, nostalgia and some emotion was already starting to invade my memories. I now knew my trip back was already more than I expected.

The Bridge at Norwich across from the railroad station.

The bridge shown here is the very bridge I walked across the day late in 1943 on my first visit to Norwich which I described on page 93. Now today, I had a nostalgic walk again across this same bridge which I had walked on my very first visit to Norwich so long ago. The building at the end of the bridge is still there were I had a light lunch. It has since been remodeled into being a nice looking bar. The bridge is painted, but the same structure and the bricks along the way are the same ones. Now in this sense, I had returned to the scenes of my youth.

On the third day evening had moved to the Half Moon Inn in Rushall, reserved for us by Ron Leigh who had driven from Manchester to visit with us.

Cambridge.

The next day Ron gave me a ride to Cambridge, showing me the many historical places. Later we visited the American Memorial Cemetery at Madingley near Cambridge and visited the grave of our navigator, Lt. Harold C. Becker, a member of our crew who had been killed by flak on a mission to Berlin on May 7th 1944, the week I had completed my tour, needless to say this was an emotional visit.

The grave of Lt. Harold C. Becker.

We had also had been invited to meet two men of the 94th Bomb Group who are engaged in planning the reconstruction of that area as a museum. When in cambridge we were near the original site of the 94th Bomb Group, therefore, we stopped in at an agreed upon time.

There we met John Adams and Cliff Fulman who introduced us around. I also lowered the flag atop the 94th Bomb Group Museum Tower. We had dinner at "The Flying Fortress,"quite a famous place near the 94th.

Duxford Airshow.

The next day Ron Leigh gave Scott and me a ride to Duxford to attend the best airshow I have ever seen as well as to visit the huge Air Museum there.

The B-17 "Sally B" at the Airshow at Duxford.
She played the "Memphis Belle" in the 1989 movie.
Note the original movie nose art.

The B-17 "Mary Alice" also displated at the at
the Airshow at Duxford.

The Main Runway.

One of the exciting events to me I recall here. One day Carol Batley took me in her car to an area which was being plowed and returned to farmland. The fascinating part to me was the huge tractor and plow was plowing the very ground on which our main runway used to be. This was the east-west long 6,300 foot runway on which we took off and landed from on most all of our missions.

Plowing the E-W Runway

The tractor shown here was huge and cost $120,000 and the six-bottom plow was $20,000. One could only imagine the work necessary to remove the heavy layer of concrete runway to return it to farmland.

While standing there, I could recall many of the takeoffs and landings we had made on this very place which once was our main runway.

There were times as we were taking off on a mission, I would look out of the radio room window and see many people standing beside the runway, some were waving as we roared past. Our pilots Capt. Van Steenis and Lt. Ogg held a speed of 140 mph as we cleared the ground, quite spectacular.

I also recall a rainy morning, we started down this runway with a full load of gas and bombs. We had a supercharger "blowout" when we were at the "point-of-no-return" on this runway.

This "blowout" caused the failure of one engine. We took off but knew we had to land and tried finding the runway in that poor visibility, it required two attempts and we finally landed and were escorted to another spare plane and again took off.

The irony being, we were flying as a spare that day. We flew out to the designated point over the North Sea and no spares were needed, and no place to fill in with the formation, no planes had dropped out. We returned to back to the base and again landed on this same runway with this full load...no mission credit, just a day of fun.

Now later "today" we actually standing on the old hardstand on which this spare plane we had used was parked that day. The concrete hardstand is yet quite intact. We stood on this place with Jim Gintner, a volunteer at the museum and Stephan Page as they had brought us to this area.

This certainly was more memories and nostalgia. I know it is one only a returning veteran can fully grasp. Now we could thank these fellows who were thoughtful enough to bring us out here for this memorial contact.

Hardstand 5, the only intact dispersal left on the base, it still has oil stains from the B-17s four engines.

I thought of the movie *Twelve O'Clock High*, showing a former veteran standing out on an abandon bomber base runway with thoughts of his experiences flooding his memory. My recollections as I stood on that area of our old runway possibly were somewhat like that scene in the movie. However, all combat crews had different experiences.

There are yet two remaining taxi strips in fair condition. One parallels the east-west runway on the north side. The other parallels the east side of the field and leads to the end were we parked our plane named "HARD LUCK!" on hardstand 29 shown on the map on page 34. Jim and Stephan gave us a ride to that area. Nothing remains of our original hardstand. Stephan found among the weeds some broken pieces of concrete which were part of the hardstand, I now have them as mementoes.

*This is one of the two remaining taxi strips, this one leads
to hardstand 29 where we parked HARD LUCK!
This photo is looking south from the intersection with the
west end of the main runway.*

*This is the other of the two remaining taxi strips,
this one runs east-west in front of the Control Tower,
hardstand 5 is on this section of taxi strip.*

To me riding now in the car on this same taxi strip which we once used was again quite a sensation. In retrospect I could recall the coughing, roaring engines of our B-17 and squealing brakes as we once had taxied along, getting in position for takeoff. Needless to say this was quite reminiscent of the days gone by.

Southwold.

Another great experience, one day I had a trip to see the shore of the North Sea. Tom Oakley, a volunteer gave me a ride in his car. We drove through the beautiful English countryside to the tourist town of Southwold, on the coast of the North Sea.

The shoreline of the North Sea at Southwold.

Tom knew I had flown over the North Sea many times. However, I had seen the sea from above from our B-17 as we often flew home from a mission alone and out of formation by choice, but never from ground level.

The sea below us then looked treacherous as it was deathly cold in the winter when we were there during the winter of 1943-44.

Then later that day I was invited to his home for dinner. I also met Mrs. Oakley then for the first time. This was another "Red Letter" day for me. To experience again this courtesy and generosity was overwhelming to me.

9-11.

We were in the Varian Center at the Museum when we heard of the tragic events unfolding in the U.S.A. We heard of the two airliners flown into the World Trade Center Towers in New York and their collapse and another airliner flown into the Pentagon in Washington D.C. and the crash of another in Pennsylvania. We were to leave on the following day, but all flights were cancelled indefinitely. Carol Batley at once invited us to stay at her home as long as necessary. This we did and it was a stay of eight days before we could get a flight home.

Our Extended Stay.

Many events occurred while we were staying with Batleys, there were many visits to the Museum and various points of interest.

From the Batley's home an old Dutch windmill is nearby. The mill still grinds flour and was built in 1860. This windmill was in the path of the bombers landing and taking off from the 100th Bomb Group base. No doubt I had flown over it many times in the past.

The windmill near the 100th Bomb Group base.

One day Mr. and Mrs. Gordon Dickie gave me a ride and a tour of the town of Diss. Many points of interest to me that would have been missed had I had not had their tour. That evening, Scott and I were invited to their home for dinner. Gordon is a volunteer at the museum.

The Brick.

While our extended visit included many trips to the museum, we were interested in seeing the area called "Site 4" which contained the buildings used by our 350th Bomb Squadron. Our barracks, Operations, latrine and many others which we were slightly acquainted with in the "old days" of World War II. As we drove out to this area we found many changes that did not conform to the memory I had of the area. The roads were blocked off. The main lane we once used to ride our bikes to main part of the field is barely recognizable.

This lane was used also for light trucks and jeeps to take us to briefings in the early mornings. Also rather than use the trucks, some of us often rode our bike instead.

Often the time was officially stated by this order, and the familiar tune of *"wake up fellows, breakfast at 2 a.m., briefing at 3 a.m.!"*

We then boarded the trucks or bikes and rode in the cold mornings to the mess hall, the cold drafty mess hall. Eating a breakfast which seemed only fair at best. Then out for a ride to the briefing rooms.

Now today, I noticed all of this area had been changed completely. Buildings we once knew were demolished, most all remnants of these were gone, only a few vacant ghostly shambled relics remain of these buildings.

I therefore, was much interested in visiting the area of our barracks where I had. With my Crew #13, lived for almost a year. Scott and I were escorted out to that area by Jim Gintner, Ron Batley and Ron Leigh.

Arriving at Site 4, it certainly was a miserable let down to my recollections of what it once was. My reflections of the area were completely lost. Nothing remained that was recognizable to me.

Although, I knew by the few landmarks we were at the correct location. Only one building, which was covered with small trees and nettles which had grown up through the interior of the building, was standing.

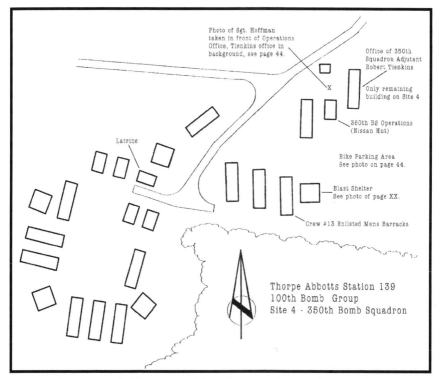

Photo of Sgt. Hoffman taken in front of Operations Office, Tienkins office in background, see page 44.

Office of 350th Squadron Adjutant Robert Tienkins

Only remaining building on Site 4

350th BS Operations (Nissan Hut)

Bike Parking Area See photo on page 44.

Latrine

Blast Shelter See photo of page XX.

Crew #13 Enlisted Mens Barracks

Thorpe Abbotts Station 139
100th Bomb Group
Site 4 - 350th Bomb Squadron

The map of Site 4 used by the 350th Bomb Squadron.

All the windows and doors were gone from this one building which was once the office of our Squadron Adjutant, now just a shell. Now to find where our barracks had once stood.

We walked along the trees and found the area which certainly was the "Bike Parking Area." From that point of reference we knew the barracks were near by.

We walked through a tangled mess of small trees, some over the years had fallen, this added to the problem of walking.

We also had to ward off the burning weed or nettles as the british call them. The walking was anything but pleasant, but curiosity goaded us on. We passed what we used to call the "blast shelter", barely recognizable with the trees growing through it.

The blast shelter next to our barracks at Site 4.

However, I recalled we used it once on a cold rainy morning 58 years ago, I told of this incident earlier on page 105.

Now I knew, as we walked on, we were nearing our barracks which was located right next to this blast shelter.

By this time the younger fellows of our group were ahead of me a short distance. However, I was struggling along. Finally I knew I was standing on the floor of our barracks, the building was completely gone.

Jim Gintner came up beside me and he and I scraped through a three-inch layer of moss and dirt, and there we found the concrete floor of the barracks!

Now I was satisfied and said *"I'm going back to the car"* which was parked in the clearing, Jim continued to explore farther out.

I could hear Scott and perhaps Ron talking in the distance as I headed back to restful seat in the car. I was all fed up with fighting the tangled mess, but had completed my desire to at least find the barracks where it had once stood.

Suddenly I heard someone shouting *"I found a brick from that barracks!"* It was the voice of Scott exuberant and glad he and Ron had found the ancient relic of that barracks as a memento of our search.

They all returned to the car as dusk was nearing and it was getting a bit dark. Scott had the brick, it was covered with dirt. We all completed what we had started out to do.

The brick from our barracks, 58 years later.

Perhaps I was more elated than any one as I had lived in that area once 58 years ago, and then of course much younger.

Memories and reflections of that past could flood ones mind as we sat there now discussing this walk through the now tangled mess. I being the only one who knew and recalled somewhat the way it was in during WWII.

All of my present companions on this trek were "youngsters." We had *"the brick"* thanks to Scott and Ron's determination to find it.

As we returned to the museum area, Scott washed off the brick and it looked quite good after it's 50 or 60 years of use. I told Scott *"now you have a memento of the barracks,"* he at once said *"this is your brick."*

Since we found the brick soon after 9-11, the airlines had restrictions on baggage, and we were concerned we couldn't take it back with us. Ron and Carol suggested leaving the brick with them and they would ship it to me later. That was the only solution to me getting the brick home.

The final step to me getting the brick is explained here. Ron and Carol attended the 100th Bomb Group Reunion at Savannah, they carried the brick with them and delivered it to Mike Faley as he was attending this reunion. He then carried it with him to his home in California and shipped it to me here in Arizona.

I finally had my brick, and now it resides on my bookshelf prominently displayed. The generosity and help of many involved is highly appreciated by me. Now as I look at a simple brick, the history of it is told here somewhat simply, but authentically.

We could ask, is it only a brick? However, to us who were looking at the old barracks site, and to all who are interested in history, it seems more than *"just a brick."*

My mind has been flooded with old memories since arriving in England. A couple that are quite vivid I will explain here.

The True Story of "Any Gum Chum?"
We had flown our B-17 from the U.S.A. to England. Landing finally at Burtonwood, England. Late September 1943.

Contrary to some military arrivals we read about or have heard about the Bands greeting the military men as the leave home or arrive at some designated place. They were often met and greeted by a Band. We seemed to have none of that in the Air Force.

We landed our B-17 and no one greeted us other than perhaps a truck or jeep came out as we parked the plane to give us a ride to the operations office. This was war, and all was a serious business, we did not expect a formal greeting of any type.

We stayed over at Burtonwood a short time as I vaguely recall, possibly overnight, then we were on our way to Bury St. Edmunds, the home of the 94th Bomb Group.

Our method of transportation was in open trucks. This was okay as we had a good view of the passing countryside. We drove slowly past several small villages.

As we drove through the villages we were surprised by several kids along the way who briefly followed our slowly moving truck. They shouted *"Hi Yank, any gum chum?"* This was all fun for us and we gave them gum or cookies or candy, what ever we had.

Now I recall this much later, it was our only greeting we had been given to England. I recently talked to one of these "kids" who told me his mother used to tell them not to be so forward, and reprimanded them for shouting at the "Yanks."

Now at last I could thank him for his part in greeting us as the first greetings we had in England. I think this greeting *"Hi Yank, any gum chum?"* became quite a national saying, well known by many. However it was our first knowledge of it on that trip to the 94th Bomb Group, that late September 1943.

Now again I can tell these "kids" who are perhaps 65-75 years old, they have done their part to give us a nice loud welcome to England.

I considered this one of the lighter moments of the war, and given to us by these enthusiastic children. This certainly raised our spirits as we were heading to a place we knew nothing about.

So now to all of you "kids" involved I can give you a belated *"Thank You"* for enthusiastically welcoming us to England.

Granack's Crew.
The crew of Lt. Frank Granack who lived in our barracks for quite some time. We were all well acquainted with these men as they were one of the older crews left in our barracks. We considered them one of the "older" crews as they were the *only* older crew left other than our own crew, since the loss of Devore's and McClain's crews who were mentioned had been lost on pages 71 and 73.

This crew flew one of the first missions to Berlin on March 4th and on that flight the flight engineer Harold Stearns had been credited with shooting down the first

German fighter over Berlin.

However, this day of March 6th they again flew to Berlin and were hit by flak which caused them to leave the]protection of the formation, by so doing they were attacked by several German fighters and eventually were shot down.

The radio operator was killed in the plane and also the tail gunner. The crew bailed out and spent the remainder of the war as POWs. This tragic flight occurred on the crew's 16th combat mission. This loss was felt by us as we returned from our nine day leave.

In the annals of war these men were among the others who also had been lost from our barracks during what was called "the week they first hit Berlin." The fortunes of war had been determined our crew would not be flying that week.

These were just a couple of memories of my time here at the 100th Bomb Group that I remembered during our extended stay now in September 2001.

The Two B-17s Assigned to Crew #13.

I will mention here the fate of our two B-17s which were assigned to Crew #13. The first one was a olive drab painted B-17F and was named "HARD LUCK!" The other was a natural metal finish B-17G, we just called it '903 or HARD LUCK! 2.

The First: B-17F #23413, HARD LUCK!

Here is the story of HARD LUCK! which I heard after I returned to the U.S.A. HARD LUCK! was shot down on August 14th, 1944 on a mission to Ludwigshafen, Germany, it was hit by flak at the IP of the bomb run.

The full story was related to me many years later by the radio operator of that flight. He had bailed out with all members of the crew as HARD LUCK! spiraled down out of control. All crew members that had bailed out landed safely and became POW's. The plane crashed and burned as it exploded on impact.

Later, I heard from a German Historian as to the exact place it landed, also saying it burned completely after exploding. It destroyed some farm buildings, and now in their place, a restaurant is located.

HARD LUCK! was lost on it's 63rd mission, it had arrived at the 100th on August 13th 1943 and was lost on August 14th 1944, a year to the day of it's arrival at the 100th Bomb Group. Sadly, on this date the famous HARD LUCK! had met it's fate.

The Second: B-17G #4231903 HARD LUCK! 2

We were assigned this brand new natural metal finish plane in the middle of March of 1944. We called it "HARD LUCK! 2." However, we did not paint the name on the nose as was done on our first plane.

Our pilot asked Sgt. Goodman, our ball turret gunner to print under the pilots window this name in honor of his wife, "Freckle Puss." That was the only painting on the plane. We only referred to it as '903.

We flew lead with this plane on several missions. We had been assigned this plane after our 17th mission and designated to fly lead using this B-17. I do not have records on how many missions we flew with this B-17.

We led several missions, one listed in the book on page 81 to Bordeaux, France as we led the group on March 27th, 1944. On April 22nd, 1944 and another flight to Hamm, Germany in which we again led the 100th Bomb Group.

We were flying '903 when I completed my tour on may 1st, 1944. Both our flight engineer and me completed that day. Tragically on May 7th, we flew the last mission of Crew #13 and on that flight our navigator Lt. Harold Becker was killed and bombardier Capt. Lester Torbett was seriously wounded.

The plane crew were fortunate in returning to the 100th Bomb Group base with two engines gone. It was a miraculous return from Berlin and also across the North Sea.

Crew #13 disbanded after that date. Three members of the crew had a few missions to complete for their official tour, which they did at later dates.

'903 was being repaired, and after a time '903 again went out on a mission dated July 29th, 1944 piloted by Eden Jones and co-pilot Robert Rids. They flew into rough opposition and '903 was shot down.

Five of the crew members were killed, including the two pilots. The four remaining crew men bailed out and were captured and became POW's.

This report explains the fate of these two B-17s to which we, Crew #13 had been assigned. Our crew had flown other B-17s in the course of out tour. However, these two were the only ones officially assigned to our Crew #13.

Seemingly strange perhaps. we did develop some sentimental association to these two B-17s. HARD LUCK! and '903, for which they had returned us safely back to the 100th Bomb group base from so many rough missions.

To us who had flown so long, it seemed these two B-17s meant more to us than just a large piece of metal. Now both planes had met the fate as had so many others, and carried with them to their end, their individual history.

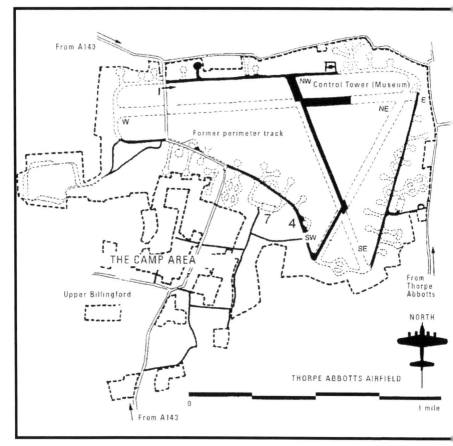

This map shows the remaining paved areas of the base.

Leaving for Home Again.

The flying restrictions to the U.S.A. were finally lifted and we were ready to go home. The day arrived for us to leave. Carol gave us a ride to Ipswich, accompanied by Gordon Dickie who came to bid us goodbye. We met Stephan Page there at Ipswich, he had again volunteered to take us to the airport in London.

The day was rainy, and a rather emotional farewell to think of leaving our new friends who had treated us with the cordiality and generosity and welcome for the time we had spent visiting England and the famous 100th Bomb Group Memorial Museum.

So finally on this rainy day, we were ready to board our Boeing 777 for the flight back home.

With again some nostalgic thoughts, as the beautiful countryside of England fading from view from my look-out point today from the window of the huge 777, I now was looking at England from the 777 instead of the deck of the ocean liner as I did on that early morning in July, 1944.

This scene seemed today much the same as it did then, 57 years ago. My thoughts again, will I ever return.

However, now this addition would not be complete if I didn't include the names of the Museum Volunteers and the visitors I met there.

The Dedicated Volunteers

Ron & Carol Batley	Ken Everett
Mrs. Gene Harvey	Tom Oakley
Gordon Dickie	Maurice Ling
Mike Plummer	Richard Gibson
Dick O'Niel	Paul Meen
John Goldsmith	Mike Nice
Jim Gintner	

The Many Visitors We Met

Stephan & John Page	Ron Leigh
Allen Harris	Robert Batley
Mr. & Mrs. Nunn	Stephan & Georgina Kingfisher
John & Beryl Bloomer	John Somerville
Ray Hubbard	Bob & Gene Timewell
Ronald Lanham	Rex White (from Wisconsin)
Marv & Jaqui Gibbons	Michael Harrowven

Martin Bowman (the author of many B-17 books)
Philip Boast

To these people I met, I say "Thank You" for our brief association on this return to Thorpe Abbotts. "You Made My Day!"

- Earl Benham

Made in the USA
Lexington, KY
11 September 2011